BECOME

*Petroc Willey teaches ethics and philosophy at Plater College, Oxford, and the Maryvale Institute, Birmingham. Katherine Willey is at present a full-time mother. This book is the result of Petroc and Katherine's meditation together on the meaning of marriage as a path to God in today's world.*

PETROC AND KATHERINE WILLEY

# BECOME WHAT YOU ARE

*The Call and Gift of Marriage*

HarperCollinsReligious
*An imprint of* HarperCollins*Publishers*

First published in Great Britain in 1992 by HarperCollinsReligious
part of HarperCollins*Publishers*
77–85 Fulham Palace Road, London W6 8JB

Printed and bound in Great Britain
by HarperCollins Manufacturing, Glasgow

*Nihil obstat* ...... Father Anton Cowan ......

*Censor*

*Imprimatur* ...... J. Crowley ......

Rt. Rev. John Crowley, V.G., Bishop in Central London.

*Westminster,* ...... 26th June, 1990. ......

The Nihil obstat *and* Imprimatur *are a declaration that a book or pamphlet is considered to be free from doctrinal or moral error. It is not implied that those who have granted the* Nihil obstat *and* Imprimatur *agree with the contents, opinions or statements expressed.*

To our parents
with love

# ACKNOWLEDGEMENTS

"The Sufficient Place" and "The Question" are reprinted by permission of Faber and Faber Ltd from *The Collected Poems of Edwin Muir*.

"The winter will lose its cold . . ." is reprinted from *Friendship and Community*, by permission of Cistercian Publications.

The extract from Psalm 95 is reprinted from *The Psalms: A New Translation* published by Wm Collins Sons and Co Ltd by permission of A.P. Watt Ltd on behalf of The Grail, England.

Scripture quotations have been taken from many different translations.

# CONTENTS

Acknowledgements 7
Preface 11
Tertullian 13

*Marriage in God*
Chosen by God 17
The Other as the Basis of Existence 22
The Image of God in Marriage 28
The Gift of Self 34
Unity is Your Vocation 39

*Living Your Vows*
Choices 47
Vowing 51
Stability 56
Conversion 61
Obedience 67

*Marriage is a Sacrament*
You are a Sacrament 75
The Mystery of Marriage 80
The Presence of God 85
A Place of Salvation 90
One Flesh 95

## *Threats to Unity*

On Guarding the Heart Against Evil Thoughts       103
Doubt       110
Anger       115
Discouragement       121
The Desire to Dominate       127

## *Living Together*

Living Simply       135
Hospitality       140
Work       145
Prayer       150
Communicating       157

Notes       163

# PREFACE

Marriage is a sacrament. It is a place where the Risen Christ meets us, inviting us to change and be redeemed. In marriage a couple encounter not only each other, but also the Lord. This book is born of the desire to understand more deeply this personal encounter with Christ in our own marriage, and to share this understanding with others.

We hope that married couples will read this book together. And we hope that it will encourage them in their lives together, as they see the tremendous dignity of their vocation. The book is designed so that it can be read in sections on a day-to-day basis, each short meditation taking only a few minutes. At the end of each chapter there are suggested readings from Scripture for further reflection. In the meditations themselves we have drawn on the experience of the whole tradition of the Church: marriage is one way to God, but every encounter with Christ can illuminate that journey. How appropriate, for example, are the monastic vows of stability, conversion of life and obedience for married life! The profound and incisive teaching of the desert Fathers, of St Augustine and St Benedict, and other Fathers and saints of the Church will therefore be found dotted around the pages. The Scripture quotations have been taken from many different translations.

We want to take this opportunity to thank all those who have inspired us by their own lives and marriages, as well as those who have supported us in our own – particularly

11

members of our family, too numerous to mention! Special thanks to the Brolly family, Breda Dwyer, Jo Gough, Father Dennis Hickley, James MacGregor, Brendan and Morwenna O'Malley, Elizabeth Moran, Karen Pizarro and Max Jnr, Jean Rooney, Marc and Teresa Schyrr, and Father Charles OFM Cap. Thanks also to Ian and Tessa MacCallum, who taught us Natural Family Planning. And many thanks to Stratford Caldecott for his helpful comments and suggestions.

Petroc and Katherine Willey
Easter 1990

# The Beauty of Christian Marriage

How beautiful . . . the marriage of two Christians, two who are one in hope, one in desire, one in the way of life they follow, one in the religion they practice. They are as brother and sister, both servants of the same Master. Nothing divides them, either in flesh or in spirit. They are, in very truth, two in one flesh; and where there is but one flesh there is also but one spirit. They pray together, they worship together, they fast together; instructing one another, encouraging one another, strengthening one another. Side by side they visit God's church and partake of God's Banquet; side by side they face difficulties and persecution, share their consolations. They have no secrets from one another; they never shun each other's company; they never bring sorrow to each other's hearts. Unembarrassed they visit the sick and assist the needy. They give alms without anxiety; they attend the Sacrifice without difficulty; they perform their daily exercises of piety without hindrance. They need not be furtive about making the Sign of the Cross, nor timorous in greeting the brethren, nor silent in asking a blessing of God. Psalms and hymns they sing to one another, striving to see which one of them will chant more beautifully the praises of their Lord. Hearing and seeing this, Christ rejoices. To such as these He gives His peace. Where there are two together, there also He is present; and where He is, there evil is not.

(Tertullian: To His Wife)

# MARRIAGE
# IN GOD

# CHOSEN BY GOD

God knew His own before they existed

\*

*God's eternal call*

The origin of your marriage lies in an eternal call from God.
From all eternity God the Father chose you both in His Son.
God knew you before the creation of the world and brought
you into existence so that, through your love for each other,
you might be sharers in His communion of love. St Paul says:
"Before the world was made, He chose us, chose us in Christ,
to be holy and spotless, and to live through love in His
presence" (Ephesians 1:4).

In the mystery of His will God chose for you both your
vocation. In the heart of God you have been saying to one
another from all eternity, "You are my beloved", "You are the
one for whom I give my life". God has chosen you to echo His
own divine conversation and mutual exchange of love. Calling
you together in His Son He has destined you to bring each
other into union with Himself, through your patience, understanding and forgiveness.

You would not seek Him or love Him unless you had first
been sought and loved. Not only in one blessing have you
been forestalled but in two, being loved as well as sought.

17

For the love is the reason for the search, and the search is the fruit of love and its certain proof.

*St Bernard of Clairvaux*

## Chosen for Love

The Lord addresses us all saying, "You did not choose Me. I chose you" (John 15:16). The Lord has chosen us for one reason: to bear fruit in plenty for the Father's glory. And the fruit He seeks from us is love: "This is My commandment: love one another" (John 15:12). We have been given a command by the Lord – there is no choice offered us to seek some other goal for our lives. God is the only reality, and His nature is perfect love; in order to be fully real ourselves, therefore, as creatures made in His image, we must be conformed to the demands of love.

Christ has chosen you to live out this universal human vocation to love in the specific form of marriage. This is a call by Christ to live at the very heart of His Church. Christ wants His people to have in their midst living images of His own relationship with His bride. You have been chosen to mirror the centre of the Church's life, her union with the Son of God.

You, my dear friends, must use your most holy faith as the foundation and build on that, praying in the Holy Spirit; keep yourselves within the love of God and wait for the mercy of our Lord Jesus Christ to give you eternal life

*Jude 20–21*

## *You are unique*

God chose for Himself a holy people, a people set apart to live for Him alone, faithful to Him, forsaking all idols. In the same way, you have been chosen by one another, chosen to live with each other for the rest of your lives. You have been called out from among all other men and women. You are set apart, holy to your spouse.

Your spouse chose you, not only for the particular qualities you have – qualities which might perhaps have been found in others – but for who you are in yourself. Your spouse has told you by their choice of you that you are unique, irreplaceable.

## *Belong to one another*

God's call to His people is a call to belong to Him exclusively, having no others beside Him (Exodus 20:5). His people are to live in His presence, faithfully observing the covenant He has made with them. In the same way, God has chosen you for each other in order that you should belong to each other, living exclusively with and for your spouse.

To belong to one another means much more than just living side by side without disturbing each other. It means being committed to becoming one flesh and one spirit; it means to live by the same values; it means identifying with each other and leaving behind all self-reliance and self-sufficiency. To belong to one another means standing side by side before the world; and it means letting go of all roles and masks which we assume to keep each other at a safe distance. This is what it means to have been chosen to belong to your spouse, under the mercy of God.

## Following the Lord

I will follow you, Lord, wherever you go
*John 13:37*

You have been chosen by the Lord: your task is to follow. This is what you promised when you married, to follow wherever the Lord might lead you. And He has made clear where He will lead you: whereas before you chose for yourselves the way you wanted to go, now you will often be carried where you have no wish to go (see John 21:18). The Lord is calling you to leave self behind, to have no care for your own safety.

You can be confident in following the Lord in this way. Your marriage is established and preserved by God and not by your power alone. It is built not so much on your natural gifts, your compatibility and your effort, as on God's faithful covenant with you both.

All Christian vocations must pass by the way of the cross, and you will certainly meet the crucified Christ in your marriage. Your marriage has been made in heaven, and those whose names are written in the book of eternal life are precisely the poor, the wounded in heart, the blind and the lame (see Luke 14:21). The Lord compels us all to set out on the long journey towards healing and wholeness. And our answer must simply be: "Lord, we have left everything to follow you" (Mark 10:28). And so there will be times when you are lonely, when you are not fully understood, when your spouse and family are not perfectly open and loving, when you do not experience the warmth for which you hoped. The Lord is calling you here to come to a deeper commitment, to learn more perfectly to love as He loves.

20

Have no fear; I have paid your ransom;
I have called you by name and you are my own.
When you pass through deep waters, I am with you,
when you pass through rivers, they will not sweep you
away

*Isaiah 43:1–2*


READINGS FOR FURTHER MEDITATION

Exodus 23:20–21
Deuteronomy 7:7–9
1 Samuel 3:1–10
Song of Songs 3:1–5
John 15:16–17
Romans 8:28–39

# THE OTHER AS THE BASIS OF EXISTENCE

"I love you", says the Lord

*Malachi 1:2*

*

## God's love for us

Our vocation in life is to be loved by God. How often we think that it is the other way around, how often we imagine that it is we who must love God first, that He waits for us to initiate any relationship. But God is the source even of our love for Him, for He is Love itself.

"The love I speak of", said St John, "is not our love for God, but the love He showed to us" (1 John 4:10). We cannot love either God or others unless we first receive the love of God; "apart from Me you can do nothing" (John 15:5).

In marriage, through each other, you begin to learn how to receive the love God has for you. You begin to learn that the Other is the basis of your existence.

## The four stages of love

One of the best expositions of the nature of love is the one set out by St Bernard of Clairvaux in his treatise, *On Loving God*. Although it deals with the love of the soul for God it is equally applicable to love within marriage.

What may seem strange at first is that his analysis of the growth of love not only begins, but also ends, with love of ourselves. Where the beginning and end points differ is in the *basis* of self-love: it is here that the real transformation takes place.

His scheme is fourfold. In the first stage we love self for self's sake; then we love God for self's sake; thirdly, we love God for His own sake; and finally we love ourselves for God's sake. It is no part of the Christian message to let go of love of ourselves, to forget ourselves and remove ourselves from the picture – we are infinitely valuable and there is no virtue in disdaining what is of such great worth. The point is to love ourselves for the right reason, to love ourselves for God's sake.

Applying this picture to marriage, the first stage is that of loving ourselves for our own sake. It is important to value ourselves because only then are we able to love others *as ourselves*. Only if you appreciate something of your own worth can you begin to appreciate the worth of another person. But if we stopped there and never loved anyone else our love, said St Bernard, would be without "justitia", without proportion. We need to love another.

And so to the second stage, which is that of loving another person for what they can do for us, in so far as they contribute to our fulfilment. From this point on our hearts gradually "expand", and we become more generous in our loving. As you experience yourself loved by another you will delight in loving in return. Slowly you begin to love your spouse for what they are in themselves and not only for what they do for you.

The final stage is where you see yourself in a new and purified light because of this love. You learn to love yourself all over again, this time for the sake of the beloved. You now love yourself "in" the total context of your marriage. You consent to being loved and make this the basis for your self-love. You accept the love your spouse has for you as the focus of your own identity, becoming aware of the beloved's gaze and knowing yourself there.

## Learning your true value

We must be *looked at* in order to be *enlightened*, and the eyes that are "bringers of light" are not only those of the divinity.

*Henri de Lubac*

The value which God places on you is your true value. This value is conveyed to you sacramentally in marriage. God has chosen you to be the incarnate gaze of love awakening the other to the realisation of their full value.

This means that, for God's will to be done in your marriage, each of you must also be open to receive the love that your spouse gives you, allowing their words of tenderness to work their way into the depths of your heart until they are fully accepted and believed. Their words of love are the words of God to you, and of these the Lord says, "so shall the word which comes from my mouth prevail; it shall not return to me fruitless without accomplishing my purpose" (Isaiah 55:11).

We have the greatest difficulty in receiving love, especially when it is offered as a free gift, as something that we have not earned. You will probably find it easier to say, "I love you", than to hear and really believe in your heart that you are loved by your spouse. But if you will not hear that you are loved then you resist allowing the beloved to become the centre of your life. You must open yourself to their love. As you do so you will realise that you are opening yourself at your point of greatest poverty and need where your whole being is characterised by a desperate longing to be filled.

## The wound of doubt

Deep within each of us is the wound of doubt as to our own value. We thirst to be affirmed for who we are, simply for the fact that we exist. As Christians, though, we believe that we are infinitely valuable to God. He has set His seal of approval upon us. We do not need to work *for* approval; we can live *from* it; for we live in Christ, in Whom God has pronounced a resounding "Yes" to each of us (see 2 Corinthians 1:20–22).

You have been given the privilege of receiving this approval sacramentally through your spouse's unconditional love for you. St Bernard urges us always to be on the alert for the "visitations" of God. For you who are married it is through each other that God visits you. Your marriage is a life-long walk to Emmaeus (Luke 24:13ff) in which both of you are to learn to recognise the presence of Christ between you so that you say, "Did we not feel our hearts on fire within us?"

## Mirroring God's love

St Catherine of Sienna said that God loves each of us as though there was only ourselves to love. He is not only the One we seek, the answer to all our yearnings; He is also our lover, and like any lover He is jealous for our good: "I, the Lord your God, am a jealous God" (Exodus 20:5). The Lord is jealous in the sense of being determined to love us, to watch over us and purge us of all evil, and to spend Himself for our good.

By its exclusiveness, your marriage reflects the nature of God's love for you. God loves each one of us as though there

25

was only us to love. In marriage you love one another in just this way, mirroring in time and space the eternity of God's passionate commitment. You affirm that your spouse has unconditional significance for you. You have singled them out from among all others and given yourself wholly to them alone.

## The Question

Will you, sometime, who have sought so long and seek
Still in the slowly darkening hunting ground,
Catch sight some ordinary month or week
Of that strange quarry you scarcely thought you sought –
Yourself, the gatherer gathered, the finder found,
The buyer, who would buy all, in bounty bought –
And perch in pride on the princely hand, at home,
And there, the long hunt over, rest and roam?

*Edwin Muir*

Since he is wise he loves you with wisdom.
Since he is good he loves you with goodness.
Since he is holy he loves you with holiness.
Since he is just he loves you with justice.
Since he is merciful he loves you with mercy.
Since he is compassionate and understanding
he loves you with gentleness and sweetness.

He loves you with the greatest humility and the deepest respect,
making himself your equal and you his equal.

He joyfully reveals his face to you
saying to you: "I am yours, completely yours.

And my happiness is to be who I am
so that I may give myself to you and be all yours".

*St John of the Cross*

READINGS FOR FURTHER MEDITATION

Psalm 139
Ezekiel 16:38
Ezekiel 23:27
Zechariah 8:2–3
Luke 24:13–35
2 Corinthians 1:20–22

# THE IMAGE OF GOD
# IN MARRIAGE

God created man in his own image and likeness: calling
him to existence through love, he called him at the same
time for love.

*Pope John Paul II*

*

### Your real face

You have a special place in creation because you are made in
God's image (Genesis 1:27). God is the creator of everything
that exists and so everything bears traces of Him, of His being
and goodness. But you, as human beings, reflect the nature of
God in a far deeper and fuller way than other creatures. You
are God's supreme work of art (Ephesians 2:10), and are
infinitely valuable to Him.

Since we are made in God's image we discover who we are
and what our nature is by understanding who God is and what
God's nature is. This is why St Paul could say: "in a word, as
God's dear children, try to be like him, and live in love as
Christ loved you" (Ephesians 5:1–2).

You are to be like God! And becoming like God will mean a
discovery of your true selves, since God is the pattern after
which you were made. Your real face is the face of Christ. You
are to love one another as Christ loves you.

28

## Made whole in each other

God has revealed Himself to us as Trinity, as three Persons in one communion of love. God is One, and this is not the oneness of a unit, but of a *union*. The unity of God arises out of the Father, the Son and the Holy Spirit existing completely for each other. Because we are made in God's image, this is where our thinking about our own human nature must start. And this is also where your understanding of your marriage must begin.

Individually we are incomplete. We are made whole only when we join ourselves to others in love and understanding. Scripture says that it is not good for a person to be alone because God has created us as two-in-one (Genesis 1:27). We are created to find our wholeness through the gift of ourselves to another. What seems like our death – giving ourselves away – is really our entrance into new life.

Any human relationship in which there is some sincere sharing of ourselves with another person reveals something of the nature of God. And marriage is one of the fullest and clearest revelations of God because in marriage we vow to give ourselves completely to each other for the rest of our lives. St John Chrysostom therefore says this about married couples:

> The two have become one. This is not an empty symbol. They have not become the image of anything on earth, but of God himself.

## Treasure your incompleteness

The Lord God caused a deep sleep to fall upon Adam, and while he slept took one of his ribs and closed up the place with flesh; and the rib which the Lord God had taken from the man he made into a woman and brought her to the man.

*Genesis 2:21–22*

This beautiful passage is of great significance for our understanding of marriage. It foreshadows the birth of the Church from the wounded side of Christ, taken from Him in the deeper sleep of death (John 19:34). We are the "new Eve", the bride of Christ, who will be brought to Him at the end of time spotless and pure (Ephesians 1:4), truly a helper fit for Him. And just as a man leaves his father and mother to join himself to his wife (Genesis 2:24), so Christ left His Father and His Father's house and made the long journey into our mortality so that He might join Himself to us as His bride. Adam was made incomplete that he might find a richer completion in Eve; but Christ made Himself incomplete for our sakes, so that He might unite us to Him and make us rich from the infinity of His gifts.

You, too, are called to find your completion in each other. You are not whole in yourselves alone, but need to receive the free gift of one another. You have married because you have realised that your wholeness can only come from outside of yourselves: you have started on the royal road of mutual dependence. Do not turn back, then, because you feel that it asks too much of you, or offends your pride, or makes you fearful because you do not have the same control over your life. Admit your weaknesses and needs freely to each other. Treasure feelings of incompleteness and even of loneliness: they are reminders that you are not self-contained.

Even as a couple you remain radically incomplete if you are without God. God is the end of all our longing, the place where all creatures find their home. Let God draw you, as a

30

couple, towards Him, "desiring to be desired, loving to be loved" (St Maximus the Confessor).

## Remade in Christ

God's image will not be formed in your marriage without much work on your part. Although we are made in the likeness of God, we have betrayed our inheritance and tried to find our identities in loves and practices below our true dignity. Our nature is godlike but all too often we act as though we were merely mortal and earthbound. We have turned away from our true nature and are now lost in the "land of unlikeness", as St Augustine put it. The pain we find in life stems from this contradiction at the heart of things – that we constantly deny who we really are.

You were made in the image of God: allow Him to remake this image in you, as He moulds you into one flesh. Those who built the Tower of Babel did so to make a name for themselves (Genesis 11:4) and because they would not accept the name God had given them (see Revelation 2:7). But they ended in alienation, unable to understand one another. You will find, in the same way, that any alienation you experience in your marriage is the result of trying to create an image for yourselves. If the Lord is not the centre of your life together you build in vain.

Christ endured the cross in order to give us back to ourselves, to enable us to return to full freedom and communion with each other. In Christ, Who is the pure image of the invisible God, we were made and have now been remade. "We all reflect as in a mirror the splendour of the Lord; thus we are transfigured into his likeness, from splendour to splendour" (2 Corinthians 3:18).

Direct one another's gaze, then, towards Christ the Lord,

31

and towards what is good and true, beautiful and noble, until God recognises the face of His only Son in your faces, lit up by the glow of the Holy Spirit.

## A spiritual discipline

The primary manifestation of the image of God in human beings is love. As St Augustine said, "You see the Trinity when you see love". And it is God's love, poured into our hearts in the gift of the Holy Spirit (Romans 5:5) which makes our love for each other possible.

Marriage is first and foremost a spiritual discipline. It is a school of love. In your marriage you can learn, hour by hour, to give up selfishness in all its forms and to consider another person as important as yourself. To love is our greatest need – to reach our true fulfilment we need someone to serve, someone to love. The service of your spouse, then, is your path to sanctification. In your marriage you will find your greatest happiness in loving one another. And through loving each other you will rise, by degrees, to love God who created and sustains you. Through love, you will embrace God who *is* love.

> God is above all love and the fount of love. The great John says this: "Love is of God" and "God is love" (1 John 4:7–8). The creator has impressed this character also on us. "By this all men will know that you are my disciples if you have love for one another" (John 13:35). Therefore, if this is not present, all the image becomes disfigured.
>
> *St Gregory of Nyssa*

God did not, on the one hand, fashion woman independently from man, otherwise man would think of her as essentially different from himself. Nor did He enable woman to bear children without man; if this were the case, she would be self-sufficient. Instead, just as the branches of a tree proceed from a single trunk, He made the one man Adam to be the origin of all mankind, both male and female, and made it impossible for men and women to be self-sufficient.

*St John Chrysostom*

READINGS FOR FURTHER MEDITATION

Genesis 1:27–28
Genesis 2:20–24
Ecclesiasticus 42:24–25
Romans 8:14–17
Ephesians 3:14–19
Colossians 1:15–20
Revelation 2:17

# THE GIFT OF SELF

The Father is in me, and I am in the Father
*John 10:38*

\*

## The gift of God

When St John says that "God is love" (1 John 4:16) he means that God is the total gift of self. God is a Trinity of giving and receiving. The Father gives Himself perfectly to the Son; the Son in turn gives Himself perfectly to the Father. This mutual self-gift is the Holy Spirit, the mutual divine love of the Father and the Son. St Basil says, "Everything that the Father is is seen in the Son, and everything that the Son is belongs to the Father. The Son in his entirety abides in the Father, and in return possesses the Father in entirety in himself".

In scripture the Spirit is called "the gift of God" and it is He who is poured into your hearts enabling you to make gifts of yourselves to one another. When you make this sincere gift of yourselves you are sharing in the life of God.

## Our deepest need

Our deepest need is to give ourselves to another. This is the centre of our being. We are made in the image of God, who is eternal self-gift, and so the most basic need we have is to make ourselves gift for another. If we do not give ourselves away we cannot find fulfilment.

34

The prophet Hosea spoke about this when he recorded how the punishment suffered by the Israelites for their rejection of God was that they would no longer be able to offer sacrifice, to give to God:

> They shall pour out no wine to the Lord,
> they shall not bring their sacrifices to him . . .
> their food shall only stay their hunger,
> it shall not be offered in the house of the Lord.
>
> *Hosea 9:4*

The Israelites had assumed that they were self-sufficient, and had looked upon God as a burden and a restriction, someone who demanded sacrifice for no good reason. They wanted to be the sole point of reference and value in life, organising and controlling everything just as they wished. Their punishment was to have this wish granted: from now on they would not be able to give themselves away, to serve anything higher than themselves; their bread would no longer be offered in sacrifice but would only satisfy their physical hunger.

The Son of God is the pattern of our lives. He receives everything that He has from the Father, and gives to others everything that He has received. Make this the pattern for your marriage. You have received all that you are from the Father and now need to give yourselves to one another and have that gift of yourselves welcomed and accepted. We suffer when we are not fully accepted because this divine impulse within us is denied. Your love for one another, therefore, will be expressed as much in gratefully receiving all that your spouse has to offer you as in giving to them. Know that their happiness lies in giving themselves to you, and do not reject their gift.

## *Sharing all things*

Christian marriage is the call to make the total gift of yourselves to each other, and the gift of your married relationship to God. You are to share all that you have and all that you are with each other, celebrating together the values of life and of love.

This means a complete sharing of possessions. St Benedict taught that in monasteries "all things should be the common possession of all". He was determined not to allow self-will in the monastery in the form of separate, jealously guarded possessions. He was echoing in his legislation what was written in the Letter of Barnabus, an early document of the Christian faith: "if you are sharers in what is imperishable, how much more in the things that perish".

You also express your love and commitment to each other through a bodily gift of self, which can in turn strengthen your spiritual unity. See in this bodily union a renewal of the covenant of love you have made with each other, a beautiful and worthy expression of love which makes visible and tangible your inner self-offering.

## *The best gift*

Heloise summed up the essence of marriage when she wrote, in a letter to Abelard, "Nihil mihi reservavi" – "I have kept nothing for myself". You are called to share not only your possessions and your bodily selves, but to consecrate the whole of your lives to one another.

You do this in imitation of Christ, who loved the Church and gave Himself to her (Ephesians 5:25). Both the Church and marriage are creations of God, communities which illuminate and reinforce each other, so that St Paul could explain the community of marriage in terms of Christ's union with the Church. Just as Christ gave Himself completely, so you have promised the best that you have, to be placed at the service of your spouse and family. Just as Christ opened His heart and gave Himself completely to the Father, so you must hold back nothing for yourself alone. It does not matter how much or how little you think you are bringing to your marriage. What matters is that you bring it all and surrender it gladly. The only gift that is really sought is the gift of yourself.

The Lord said, "Is there a man among you who will offer his son a stone when he asks for bread, or a snake when he asks for fish? If you, then, bad as you are, know how to give your children what is good for them, how much more will your heavenly Father give good things to those who ask him!" (Matthew 7:9–11). Like any parent, God wants the best for His children. And so He has chosen you as the best gift He could give to the person who is now your spouse.

## *Lay down your lives for each other*

In the eternal counsels of God the decision to create already involved the incarnation, crucifixion and descent into hell of the Son of God. The Lamb of God was slain from the foundation of the world because of the foreseen fall of humanity and the angels (Revelation 13:8). The sacrifice of the Son has its origin in the timeless life of the Trinity.

This sacrifice is God's supreme act of love for us, because He takes into Himself the depths of human sin and loneliness. The Son "became sin" for our sake (2 Corinthians 5:21), and took upon Himself the full effects of that sin. On the cross God stripped Himself of the seamless garment of His unity, and we see there the Trinity loving even in the depths of despair and estrangement. The Father and the Son are

37

hidden from each other, are at an infinite distance from each other, and yet remain trusting and committed even in that distance. Jesus prays, "Into thy hands I commit my spirit" (Luke 23:46).

In the image of this God of ours, you must be ready to love your spouse even in ways that are costly and involve great sacrifice on your part. Make the sign of the cross often, to remind yourselves that it is indeed a costly thing to love as God loves. In your marriage you will be asked to carry one another's burdens, and in the most ordinary but real way to lay down your lives for each other.

This is God's love: to take pains for each other.

*Pachomius*

READINGS FOR FURTHER MEDITATION

Numbers 18:29
Matthew 5:23–26
John 3:16
John 15:10–15
2 Corinthians 5:18–6:1

# UNITY IS
# YOUR VOCATION

May they be one, even as we are one.

*John 17:22*

\*

*Restored to unity*

Marriage is a call to unity. Above all else, this is your vocation. You are to become one heart and one soul before God. This is what God is working in your marriage to bring about.

At the Fall, the unity which existed between man and woman, between humanity and God and between humanity and nature was broken. Sin shattered a harmonious whole, so that now we fight and destroy each other, seeking our own good without thinking of our spouse. Instead of a deep unity resulting from mutual self-giving we find that marriages can be torn apart by domination, recrimination, the quest for power and spouses falsely seeking fulfilment apart from each other. "Satan has broken us up" (St Cyril of Alexandria).

Christ's work is one of restoration. He came to unite what was divided, making peace by His death on the cross. All enmity between man and woman has been destroyed by His victory on the cross. Unity is possible once more.

Your lives are now hidden with Christ in God (Colossians 3:3), and it is in Christ that you will discover the full significance of your marriage. Your old lives, lives of separ-

39

ateness, are dead. The angels who guarded the way to paradise (Genesis 3:24) now sit at the entrance of His tomb
showing the way to a new life. Let the power and love of
Christ, then, transform your life together so that you become
one flesh and one spirit. If you die with Him, leaving your old
selves behind, you will rise to this new life, united as one flesh
in His risen body.

> We who were sundered and at enmity by reason of our
> sensuality and the diverse desires and uncleanness of our
> sins, being cleansed by the Mediator, should set out
> together towards that same blessedness, and being
> forged together into one mind by the fire of love, be
> united, not in our common nature alone but by the bond
> of a common love.
>
> *St Augustine*

## The Lord's prayer

Let God's unity be the model for the unity you are seeking
with each other. The unity of God lies in the loving communion of Father, Son and Spirit, who are eternally giving
themselves to each other. God has joined you together in
marriage so that you might mirror this union of perfect love.
Father, Son and Spirit are not three separate wills, three
different centres of being. There is only one will, in which the
three Persons share. You, too, must bind yourselves to live in
agreement with each other, making unity your absolute priority (see Philippians 2:2). The Lord's prayer for you is that
this unity between you might become a reality:

> The glory which thou gavest me I have given to them,
> that they may be one, as we are one; I in them and thou in

me, may they be perfectly one. Then the world will learn that thou didst send me, that thou didst love them as thou didst me.

*John 17:22–23*

Satan will try to divide you, for he knows that a household divided against itself cannot stand (Luke 11:18). We rightly call him diabolic – that is, one who separates, who divides into two. So put on all the armour that God provides, so that you are able to stand firm against him. Be open and sincere with each other, with unity as your aim, and the devil will find no resting place in your home.

## You are one body

Toil together, wrestle together, run together, suffer together, rest together, rise together.

*St Ignatius of Antioch*

The Scriptures describe unity in marriage in the strongest possible terms: "A man leaves his father and mother and clings to his wife, and the two become one flesh" (Genesis 2:24). The man does not just live with his wife – he *clings* to her; they do not simply live closely together – they become *one flesh*. In loving each other, St Paul says, you love yourselves, for you are one body (Ephesians 5:28); and if one suffers, both suffer together (1 Corinthians 12:26), for there is no separation between you. St Paul even says that the holiness of one, because of the closeness of your union, makes both of you holy before God (1 Corinthians 7:14).

The unity of husband and wife is the fundamental basis for family unity. The Lord honours the marriage unity even above that of parent and child. As husband and wife you are

41

completed in each other, two halves finding your completion in a single whole. As mother and father you must let your children go if they want to marry because their completion lies not in you but in another.

## Making space for the new

Your unity with each other is made possible only by a break with the past. A man must leave his father and his mother and be united with his wife. And with regard to the woman, the psalmist says, "Listen my daughter, hear my words and consider them: forget your own people and your father's house" (Psalm 45:10). When you married you entered a new way of life and left behind the old. "Here and now I am doing a new thing", says the Lord (Isaiah 43:19). God is creating something new in your lives: make space in your hearts for it. It is only possible for husband and wife to be truly united when both have left their parents and given themselves whole-heartedly to their spouse. Your real roots lie not in the past, but in God. The path to Him which He has chosen for you is marriage.

At the same time, your unity as a couple is the basis for a wider unity. Through the vow of love you have made to each other your families, also, are invited to be committed to each other. Marriage is an act of faith that not only is a bond between two original strangers possible, but that whole families can come together as well. And through any children you may have, the visible embodiment of your unity, the families are drawn together even more as they take on new responsibilities and become grandparents, aunts and uncles. In this way, as St John Chrysostom says, "the love of husband and wife is the force that welds society together".

## The Lord's yoke

Unity in marriage is not just an agreement to live together in peace and harmony, respecting one another's views and values. Nor is it simply a matter of feeling close to one another. It is a commitment you both make to establish the same priorities, the same values. It is to be united, above all, in your love for God. "Nothing is so conducive to unity", said Dorotheus of Gaza, "as rejoicing about the same things and holding to the same purpose".

The Lord has yoked you together (Matthew 11:29) so that you might walk alongside each other. So let neither of you run ahead of the other, or turn off down a different track, but walk the way of Christ side by side. Then His yoke will be good to bear and the burden light, and when one of you stumbles there will be someone to help you up again.

When in his blessing he bequeathed all power to his disciples, in his prayer to his Father he bestowed on his followers all good gifts, and he added the greatest gift of all, that they should never be fragmented or divided by a multiplicity of choices in their judgement concerning what was right, but they should all be one, united in growth with the one and only good.

*St Gregory of Nyssa*

READINGS FOR FURTHER MEDITATION

Genesis 2:21–25
Psalm 133
Matthew 11:28–30
John 17

# LIVING YOUR
# VOWS

# CHOICES

Stop at the crossroads; look for the ancient paths; ask, "Where is the way that leads to what is good?" Then take that way and you will find rest for yourselves.

*Jeremiah 6:16*

\*

## The school of marriage

God's call always seeks a response in us. He asks for our personal commitment to His plan for us. The Lord seeks us out and asks us just one question: "Do you yearn for life?" When you said, "I do" to one another in the marriage service you were also saying "I do" to this invitation to new life.

Seeking this new life, you have become disciples in a school of the Lord's service, the school of marriage, as your way to that life. No doubt you chose to marry only after much thought, and even then with a certain fear in case you should fail to live up to the high ideals it placed before you. You can be certain of God's help throughout your marriage, for having called you to this state of life His grace will never be lacking. And so St Benedict tells us never to despair of the mercy of God, and St Leo, also, reassures us saying, "The one who confers the dignity will give the strength".

## Leaving everything

Whenever we make a serious choice we have to give up

47

something in order to do or to be something else. Because we are limited creatures, who cannot do everything, our lives are marked by the constant necessity for choice. We cannot walk down all paths; we have to choose just the one that seems best. This fact gives our lives a sacrificial character, since we make a sacrifice whenever we give up something we recognise as good for the sake of what is even better. When you made the choice to marry you sacrificed your lives as single people for the sake of the higher unity of living as two-in-one-flesh. You made the choice to die as single people so that you might be reborn as a married couple.

Your willingness to have made this sacrifice is a sign of the value you place on the vocation you have embraced, for the more you value something the more you are willing to give up in order to have it. You have shown how completely you value one another by your making each other the focus of your lives. Just as Christ left everything so that He might win His bride, becoming our paschal sacrifice, so you have left everything for the sake of belonging to one another.

### Even the holiest have doubts

Having firmly committed yourselves, you will find stability in life through remaining faithful to your vocation no matter what alterations take place in your external circumstances.

Do not be like those who, in their hearts, remain un-committed, who do not make a true gift of themselves, because they think that this is the way of being free in life. Freedom is not found in lack of commitment, in keeping one's options open: that way leads only to isolation and to slavery to our desires. If you remain at a distance from life you remain also at a distance from yourself, you will never know yourself or face real challenges to grow morally and spiritually. St John of the Cross says, "The soul whose will is torn between trifles is like water which never rises because it is running through an outlet down below".

St Bernard believed that even the holiest of people have doubts about their vocation at times, but tells us that if we have made our choice in openness to God's will, and using our natural intelligence, we ought to be faithful to the decision we have made. So remain firm, finding your true dignity in meeting the challenges this way of life makes upon you. The choices you make now in your day-to-day life together should always confirm and support your marriage. Only by excluding the many fleeting and superficial opportunities you have in favour of being true to the full meaning of your marriage will you grow in moral and spiritual stature.

## God saw our beauty

There are many reasons why we draw back from giving ourselves completely to one another and to God: we are wounded in many ways, and we may also feel that the gift we have made of ourselves in the past was not valued. But all really deep relationships demand that at some point we make an act of surrender, of abandonment. The choices we make which involve another person must always be made to some extent in the dark, for every person is a mystery known fully only to God. You must trust that the beauty and goodness you have seen in the other person is their deepest reality, the radiance of God in them.

Because He saw our beauty, God committed Himself completely to loving us in His Son, so that He might finally rejoice in us, a Bridegroom rejoicing in His bride. Entrust yourselves to one another, then, letting go of your doubts, and entrust yourselves together to the Spirit who never for a moment abandons you.

The winter will lose its cold, the snow will be without
                    whiteness,
The night without darkness, the heavens without stars,
        the day without light,
The flower will lose its beauty, all fountains their water,
        the sea its fish,
The tree its birds, the forest its beasts, the earth its harvest –
All these will pass before anyone breaks the bonds of our
    love,
and before I cease caring for you in my heart.

May your days be happy in number as flakes of snow,
May your nights be peaceful, and may you be without
    troubles.

*A Cistercian monk*


READINGS FOR FURTHER MEDITATION

Deuteronomy 30:15–20
Luke 12:8–9
Luke 14:28–30
Revelation 3:14–22

# VOWING

If you voluntarily make a vow to the Lord your God, mind what you say and do what you have promised.

*Deuteronomy 23:23*

*

## *What God has joined*

When you made your vows on the day of your marriage you were doing much more than making simple promises towards one another. After all, there are many occasions when we promise to do something but find it difficult to keep to our original plan. We know that people will understand if we do not keep a prior agreement to meet if something more pressing appears unexpectedly on our horizon. We make and remake our obligations and even some of our more solemn promises. There are few commitments to which we feel unshakably bound. Most of the time we are in control of our obligations; we do not allow them to control us.

Your marriage vows are different. You made them as something absolutely binding on you. A vow is not a prediction; nor is it a hopeful expectation. When you vowed to live faithfully together for the rest of your lives you were not simply predicting or hoping that this would be the case. You were guaranteeing a lifetime's commitment to each other. You made the choice enshrined in this act of vowing the last word on the subject for you. When you made your vows you gave over your lives to each other, putting yourselves at one another's service. And at this moment your spiritual identity changed: in the eyes of God (and what He sees is the only true vision) you became inseparably joined, two spirits living as one.

## Study the Church's teaching

St Benedict said that before making his vows the prospective monk must have had the monastic rule read to him several times. In this way he can know exactly what obligations he is understanding and can make his decision after careful reflection and with full knowledge. Before making his commitment he will understand the meaning of the monastic life as fully as possible, including "all the hardships and difficulties that will lead him to God".

In the same way it is important to recognise that Christian marriage means offering yourself to another individual in the context of a particular state of life within the church. You have vowed to live together in the institution of marriage, and this means honouring the objective purposes of married life – the procreation and education of children, unity in love, and seeking God through the grace He gives in the sacrament of marriage. The church has a rich tradition from which you can draw your understanding of this noble vocation. This tradition is your inheritance, carefully guarded by the successors to St Peter and the other apostles. Study the teachings of the church on marriage and live out those teachings in your life together so that you "shine like stars" (Philippians 2:15) in a world which is seeking the light of Christ.

## *Love grows with freedom*

Marriage is inseparable from freedom. To marry, not only did you have to understand what it was you were understanding, you also had to freely say "yes" to marriage and to each other. St Benedict is equally insistent that any decision to enter the monastery must be made completely freely so that the vows reflect an inner state of commitment. Then, having made his decision, the monk must be aware that "from this day he is no longer free to leave the monastery, nor to shake from his neck the yoke of the rule which, in the course of so prolonged a period of reflection, he was free either to reject or to accept".

God never overpowers us; He never forces His designs on us against our will. He never manipulates us or compels our response. He always seeks a free return of love from us. He can only become flesh in us if we, like Mary, utter the full and free consent of our being. So also, authentic love will only continue to grow between you, making you more and more one flesh, if you respect one another's integrity, knowing that the marriage covenant can be renewed daily only by a free gift of the self.

## *Love without limits*

You have been drawn to love one another by the goodness and worth you have seen in each other. You know that this worth is infinite, that your spouse's value is beyond measure. And so you have committed yourself to this person for life, knowing that the only adequate response to the value you have perceived is the gift of all that you are and all that you have.

To love without this total commitment would be a contradiction in terms – it would have been saying that the worth of the person you have married could be measured and only deserved a limited amount of your time. You have declared that your love is immovable and will never fail, because this is the measure of their value.

My love shall be immovable and never fail
*Isaiah 54:10*

## Exchanging rings

When you made your vows you exchanged rings as signs of the faithfulness you promised. You wear a ring as a constant reminder of this conversion to the values of married life. St Francis de Sales writes this about the meaning of rings in marriage:

Of old, seals were engraved upon rings which were worn on the fingers, as Scripture itself testifies; this, then, is the explanation of the marriage ceremony: the Church, by the hand of the priest, blesses a ring, and by giving it first to the man testifies that she closes up and puts a seal upon his heart by this Sacrament, so that neither the name nor the love of any other woman may ever enter into it, so long as she lives, who has been given to him in marriage; then the bridegroom puts the ring on the finger of the bride, that she likewise may know that her heart must never entertain any affection for another man so long as he lives upon the earth, whom our Lord has just given to her.

The ring is also a circle, which is a sign of the love flowing between the Father, the Son and the Holy Spirit: God is lifting you up to share in this eternal circle of love. The rings are signs of His favour, as He welcomes you into communion with Him, just as the father welcomed home his son, putting a

ring on his finger, when he returned home from the far
country (Luke 15:22).

They are made of gold, which is a sign that you have
pledged a commitment to each other which is incorruptible,
even in the fire of testing: as Scripture says, "like gold in the
furnace He tried them" (Wisdom 3:6). Over time your ring
will become scraped and battered and may lose its superficial
beauty, just as you yourselves will be bruised by life's trials.
But by meeting these with courage and in a spirit of unity your
love will be cleansed of impurities. Slowly you will be shaped
and moulded by the hand of God until you come together to
fit into the place for which He has destined you, in His city,
made of pure gold (Revelation 21:18)

## God's support in our vowing

This is no slight matter, no easy goal; but he who, in his
love, makes you such promises is almighty and good. He
will be faithful in fulfilling them and untiring in giving
help. To those who in their great love for him pledge
themselves to great things and, believing and trusting in
his grace, undertake what is beyond their own strength,
he imparts both the will and the desire; and he follows up
the grace to will by bestowing also the power to achieve.

*William of St Thierry*

READINGS FOR FURTHER MEDITATION

Genesis 28:20–22
Ecclesiasticus 5:4
Malachi 2:13–16
Mark 10:1–12
Revelation 21:18

# STABILITY

Rooted in the Other in the other

You are built upon the foundation laid by the apostles and prophets, and Christ Jesus himself is the foundation-stone.

*Ephesians 2:20*

*

## *No looking back*

Benedictine monks and nuns take a vow of stability. This is a commitment to persevere in the search for God in the community they have joined. They remain in one community for life, certain that they will find God there.

You, also, have made a vow of stability, to persevere in the search for God with one another. You have vowed to remain together for better or for worse until death parts you. Stability for you means the total acceptance that it is with each other that you will find God. You, too, can be certain that God, who started this good work in you, will bring it to completion (Philippians 1:6).

Now that you have made your vows, realise that this is how the Lord is leading you to Himself. There are other ways to God, but for you it is this way. Living with one another in the married state – this is your specific way: "this door opens the way to God" (Psalm 118:20). Carry straight along this road, for "no one who puts his hand to the plough and then keeps looking back is fit for the kingdom of God" (Luke 9:62). So look neither to right nor to left.

At times you may be tempted to believe that you have made a mistake in vowing stability, that you married the wrong person, or should not have married at all. At such times, call on the Lord to save you, and resolve again firmly to live in faith that this is your path to God. Call on the Holy Spirit, asking Him to be with you on your journey together, to guide you in safety around all obstacles and hazards. Above all, be confident that nothing can separate you from the love of God in Jesus (Romans 8:38–39). As St Augustine said, even the hardness of our hearts is no barrier to Him: Christ passed through locked doors to give His word of peace.

## Dwell in one another

Marriage is both a gift and a task. The gift is of another person who has entrusted the whole of their life to you, and of Christ Himself, made present in this self-offering. The task is to grow into a perfect unity of love that has its source and completion in God.

Penetration into the full truth about marriage and into the depths of the other person requires fidelity over time. This is why stability is so important in marriage. You both bear the imprint of eternity and are therefore essentially mysteries to each other. It is only gradually that the full riches of yourselves to each other can be yielded up, as you grow together into a spiritual dwelling for God (Ephesians 2:22).

You are called to be stable together, but not to be static. Change and growth are signs of life, and so your stability is not an attempt to frustrate change in yourself or your spouse; nor is it the evasion of challenges for the sake of a quiet life. You are stable so that there is a definite context within which your maturing can take place. You have made a commitment of love to remain with and support your spouse *through* change. The Lord says to you, in one another, "Dwell in me, as I in you", for by dwelling faithfully in one another you will bear much fruit.

## Perseverance

The outward sign of stability is perseverance. In St Benedict's time there were monks – the Gyrovagues – who were forever roaming from place to place. St Benedict, on the contrary, insisted on stability, on perseverance in a single community. He felt that if the monk constantly changed community he would never spiritually mature. He must have the courage to stop running away from situations he finds difficult.

The Desert Fathers, also, advised monks to remain in their cells. There, they said, they would learn all they needed to know. There they would find God.

A brother asked an old man, "What shall I do, father, for I am not acting like a monk at all, but I eat, drink and sleep, carelessly, and I have evil thoughts and I am in great trouble, passing from one work to another and from that work to the next". The old man said, "Sit in your cell and do the little you can, untroubled. For I think that the little you can do now is of equal value to the great deeds which Abba Anthony accomplished on the mountain"

Be assured, then, that by remaining stable in the face of boredom, lethargy and the lack of any obvious fulfilment, by doing just the little that you can, you, like the brother in the story, will be performing deeds of the same value as Anthony, the father of monks.

## Rely on the Lord

Your perseverance will be manifested in times of hardship and trouble. As a couple you will face many difficulties out of your control – there may be problems at your work or in your families; you may not have adequate accommodation; or you may discover that you cannot have children. St Benedict writes of the monk that even under severe difficulties "his heart quietly embraces suffering and endures it without weakening or seeking escape". And he quotes Scripture for our encouragement: "Anyone who perseveres to the end will be saved" (Matthew 10:22), and again, "Be brave of heart and rely on the Lord" (Psalm 27:14).

At these times the structured life marriage provides will be able to hold your hearts firm, and relieve you of the necessity of having to act always out of the resources of your own variable feelings. They can also be times when you draw closer to support each other, realising that your love for each other is a decision you have made, an act of the will. Then, even in your sadness you can recognise with joy that "there is nothing love cannot face; there is no limit to its faith, its hope and its endurance" (1 Corinthians 13:7).

## The Rock

When they were lost in the desert God told the Israelites to strike a rock, out of which flowed water to quench their thirst (Exodus 17:7). Out of the hardness of the rock came water, the source of life. In the same way, out of the firm rock of stability life will flow into your marriage.

The rock also prefigures Christ, who gives us living water to drink, and who is the source of our stability. He is the rock, the secure base on which your marriage is founded. You can say with the psalmist, then, "In truth he is my rock of deliverance, my tower of strength, so that I am unshaken" (Psalm 62:6). You can rest your lives on the certainty of His love for you, knowing that even if you are unfaithful, He remains faithful (see 2 Timothy 2:13). He is the friend and presence in marriage who is always ready to provide you with the grace you need to live as He asks. Make Christ, then, the centre of your marriage and the foundation of your life together.

> Since Jesus was delivered to you as Christ and Lord, live your lives in union with him. Be rooted in him; be built in him; be consolidated in the faith you were taught.
>
> *Colossians 2:6–7*

And stay close in your beliefs and practice to the Lord's chosen one, Peter, "the rock", on whom He founded His church. See how in all these ways the Lord is providing us with His support and unfailing care. "You have been a safe place to live in, for us, O Lord, throughout all generations" (Psalm 90:1).

> May the Lord
> make your hearts firm,
> so that you may stand before our God and Father
> holy and faultless when our Lord Jesus Christ
> comes with those who are His own.
>
> *1 Thessolonians 3:13*

READINGS FOR FURTHER MEDITATION

Isaiah 30:15–18
Psalm 62
Psalm 127
Colossians 2:6–7
Jude 24–25

# CONVERSION

## Seeking the Other in the other

Abba Poeman said concerning Abba Pior that every day he made a new beginning.

\*

### Seeking God

The monk is asked just one question before he joins the monastic community: "Do you truly seek God?" This same question is addressed to you at the beginning of your marriage. Affirming that he does desire God with all his heart the monk takes the vow of *coversatio*. This is simply a vow of commitment to a specific way of life – for the monk, of course, the monastic way of life. On your part, you are committed to the vocation of marriage. Both are tried and tested spiritual paths to God.

St Benedict writes to reassure the new monk,

Do not be daunted immediately by fear and run away from the road that leads to salvation. It is bound to be narrow at the outset. But as we progress in this way of life and in faith, we shall run the path of God's commandments, our hearts overflowing with the inexpressible delight of love.

Your marriage, too, may seem narrow at the beginning. But it also will lead to salvation if you enter upon it with hearts full of a generous love of God and one another.

Marriage is a path, not a settled state. It is not a settling down, but the beginning of a journey, when you leave behind your former self, whether good or bad. Just as the Israelites heard the call to leave Egypt where they were in bondage, so you have been called to set out together on the road to the promised land.

God Himself is your goal. He Himself is the land you seek, a land of eternal beauty and peace. So your way has an end; it is not an aimless wandering. The Lord has called you together for a purpose, not so that you may die in the desert. Forget what is behind you, then, and reach out for what lies ahead, for the Lord is leading you to union with Himself, to be filled with all the fullness of God.

> There we shall rest and see, we shall see and love, we shall love and we shall praise. Behold what shall be in the end without end! For what other thing is our end, but to come to that kingdom of which there is no end?
>
> *St Augustine*

## Continual conversion

Your life together must be one of continual conversion. The full return to God is a lifelong task. William of St Thierry said that "No one is allowed to remain long in the same condition. The servant of God must always either make progress or go back; either he struggles upwards or he is driven down to the depths". We want to change once and for all, to be perfect immediately; we are tired of struggle. But growth in virtue is a gradual process, and we gain the fruit of humility as we strive to turn single good acts into habits and habits into character traits. Every day we have to make a fresh beginning in this work, until Christ is fully formed in us.

In our journey the Lord desires above all that we be utterly dependent on Him, and be dependent on each other as well, recognising our need. Only then does He desire our perfection. And so Abba Anthony used to say, "The greatest thing a man can do is to throw his faults before the Lord and to expect temptation to his last breath".

Be patient, therefore, with each other and with yourselves, as the Lord is patient with you. Be happy to feel your own weakness so that you may experience the power and care of God in the encouragement you receive from one another.

## Fellow travellers

Your vocation is a great and responsible one. When you married you received the life of another person. Just as Christ freely laid down His life for those He loved, so your spouse has laid down their life for you. You have been entrusted with one made in God's own image. As St Ignatius of Antioch said,

> You are all fellow travellers, God-bearers and temple-bearers, Christ-bearers and bearers of holiness.

Be ready, then, as fellow travellers, to do all in your power to assist each other in your pilgrimage towards God. You do not have to be everything for each other: only God is your total fulfilment. Your task is to accompany each other on the way, standing before the Father and interceding for one another.

Be for each other a rule of goodness, a living book in which can be read the Word of God as something alive and active.

Bring the good news to each other in word and example, binding up each other's wounds, and pointing one another beyond the shadows and distractions of this life to that better country (Hebrews 11:16) towards which the whole Church is on pilgrimage.

## Willing to be changed

The outward sign of the vow of conversion is a ready willingness to change anything in yourself and your behaviour which threatens your unity together. "With us unanimity and concord should not on any account be broken" (St Cyprian). Unity is your rule of life. To preserve and deepen this unity may require fundamental changes of attitude and a sincere effort at establishing ways of acting which place your spouse and your marriage at the centre of your life.

Always think about changing yourself before changing your spouse. Remove the log from your own eye before attending to the splinter in the eye of your husband or wife. But if your spouse is acting in a way that hurts, worries or offends you, tell them how you feel, or else resentment may follow. Your vocation is to live as two-in-one-flesh and this unity is the fruit of close and honest communication. Speak the truth to each other in love.

Without demanding change from each other, or setting conditions on your love, firmly believe that change is always possible for both of you, because with God all things are possible. Put your trust in His power to transform your lives.

## The Beginning and the End

The Son of God is the Way, and so He is the path on which you walk. He is also the Truth, and so all your seeking has its end in Him. He is the beginning and the end and the way itself.

You are travelling towards Him but in a sense you already possess Him in one another. In the sacrament of marriage Christ is already present. But you cannot possess Christ perfectly in this life. Even as you call out, "Stay with us, for evening draws on", He vanishes from your sight. In this earthly life you hold Christ by faith and move towards Him by loving rather than by walking. "Not our feet but our moral character carries us nearer him" (St Augustine). You run towards Him and towards your heavenly home by loving each other with all your heart, with all your soul and with all your might.

## A Celtic Blessing for the Journey

May the road rise to meet you.
May the wind be always at your back.
May the sun shine warm upon your face,
the rains fall soft upon your fields and,
until we meet again,
May God hold you in the palm of his hand.

. . . see and understand the difference between presumption and confession, between those who see the goal that they must reach, but cannot see the road by which they are to reach it, and those who see the road to that blessed country which is meant to be no mere vision but our home . . . It is one thing to descry the land of peace from a wooded hilltop and, unable to find the way to it, struggle on through trackless wastes where traitors and runaways, captained by their prince . . . lie in wait to attack. It is another thing to follow the high road to that land of peace.

*St Augustine*

READINGS FOR FURTHER MEDITATION

Jeremiah 24:6–7
Luke 10:1–2
John 14:1–6
Philippians 3:12–14
Hebrews 11:13–16

# OBEDIENCE

Listening to the Other in the other

Christ humbled Himself, and in obedience accepted
even death – death on a cross

*Philippians 2:8*

\*

## *Giving up self-will*

Obedience is at the very heart of the Christian revelation. It is
a quality of God Himself: the Son gives the Father an eternity
of loving obedience. Obedience was the keynote of Jesus' life.
He said, "I have come down from heaven, not to do my own
will, but the will of him who sent me" (John 6:38), and,
"Whatever the Father does the Son does likewise" (John
5:19).

Jesus and the Spirit, said St Irenaeus, are like the two hands
of the Father, for they are completely obedient to His bidding.
It is these hands of the Father Who have created and formed
each of us – "Your hands moulded me and made me what I
am" (Psalm 119:73). We have been created to live in unity
with God through a life of loving obedience.

The various states of life open to the Christian have different ways of living out this obedience. In marriage, the spouses
are obedient to each other: this is the way in which your
obedience to God is made concrete and personal. It is not
enough to profess obedience in the abstract – without action it

is useless. Jesus said, "Not everyone who calls me, 'Lord, Lord' will enter the kingdom of heaven, but only those who do the will of my heavenly Father" (Matthew 7:21). Obedience is vital for our lives, then, for it is the fundamental way in which each of us can give up self-will and self-absorption. You may ask: "Is not love, rather than obedience, the surest way to do this?" But we easily confuse love with its counterfeits, with desire and sentimentality; whereas obedience cannot be mistaken for anything else: it is as clear as glass, and as hard as stone.

In practice, obedience means four things. First it means really listening to your spouse, putting your husband or wife first in your life. Secondly, obedience should be practised at all times, and that means especially in the small, everyday events of your life – you are being obedient, for example, when you help your wife in the kitchen when you would rather be relaxing. Thirdly, if you have the spirit of obedience you will not be hesitating, but respond without delay. This expresses your genuine love for your spouse. Finally there should be no grumbling, for the Lord loves a cheerful giver.

## *Dependence*

> Naked I came from my mother's womb,
> naked I shall return whence I came.
> The Lord gives and the Lord takes away;
> blessed be the name of the Lord
>
> *Job 1:21*

We are utterly dependent upon God. That is the absolute truth of our lives. We gain joy and liberation when we recognise that fact and gladly live by it. Then we know that at every moment we exist only because we are continually loved into being by God. We know that everything we have, we have received from Him. There is nothing we have which He does not give us. The air, our food, our belongings, the people in our lives, our minds and thoughts, our prayer: all is pure gift.

God is the source of all that exists, and we receive His life through the world around us and through other people: because we have bodies we participate in a continuous flow of matter; and we reach maturity – spiritually, emotionally and intellectually – only with the constant help of other people. Dependence is the truth of our lives.

But we rebel against this truth. We do not want to be limited by others. We feel that we are only free when our first allegiance is to ourselves, when we do not have to take other people into consideration. This was the sin of our first parents: they wanted to be independent – even of God – and to steer their own way through life. But "Man is slave to that by which he wishes to find happiness", wrote St Augustine, and death entered the world, setting the seal upon our slavery, when Adam rejected dependence. Death continues to remind us that life is beyond our control.

If you want to find happiness just for yourself in your marriage, then it will quickly become sterile. The path to true happiness lies only in obedience, which means joyfully accepting that life only comes into your marriage through the mutual surrender you make to one another.

## Listening

The word "obedience" comes from the Greek "to listen". It means to hear with your heart, to be attentive to what is unspoken as well as to what is spoken. Just as we listen to the voices within ourselves, voices of happiness and contentment

69

and of sadness and dissatisfaction, so we must attune ourselves to what our spouse is saying to us.

To be able to listen well you need to be able to leave yourself behind, to let go of your worries and anxieties about yourself. For this to happen, the field of your heart needs to be ploughed by the love of God. The hard surface of selfishness must be "softened with showers" (Psalm 65:10). The Lord promised that He would do this: "I will sprinkle clean water on you", He said; "I will take the heart of stone from your body and give you a heart of flesh" (Ezekiel 36:25–26). Christ wants to cure the deafness of your heart so that you can really hear what He is saying to you in your spouse. You will then be able to let go of your own insecurity and be open to the pain and confusion your spouse feels. When your heart is open, the words your spouse speaks will fall on good soil: you will "hear the word and welcome it" (Mark 4:20) and it will bear much fruit in your marriage.

## Mutual obedience

> Be subject to one another out of reverence for Christ
> *Ephesians 5:21*

All Christian marriages look to the relationship between Christ and the Church as the model for their own. Christian married couples understand themselves and their significance in the light of the true Bride and Bridegroom, the Church and Christ. This is what it means to call your marriage a sacrament: that your primary calling is to represent Another.

The vocation of the Christian wife, therefore, is to be "holy and without blemish" (Ephesians 5:27), cleansed by the word of Christ in her innermost being. Obedient to her husband, she is totally committed to him and to the unity of the marriage. The Christian husband, on his part, is called to be obedient to his wife, "out of reverence for Christ". He knows that his is the magnificent vocation of loving his wife as Christ loved the Church. He is to provide and care for her and give himself to her without reserve, just as Christ gave Himself for the Church.

When making decisions about their marriage, neither husband nor wife act unilaterally: in their life together their highest priority is to live as two-in-one. But it is not some natural consensus of opinion they seek, but unity springing from their mutual love of the Lord. Together, both look to Christ as the head of their marriage, as their Saviour and supreme authority.

## The spirit of obedience

Obedience is often painful, because any giving up of our will is painful, until through the practice of obedience we find ourselves at peace in all things. Christ Himself "learned obedience in the school of suffering" (Hebrews 5:8), and "in obedience accepted even death" (Philippians 2:8). And so St Bernard writes, "From those things which he suffered we mere men may learn how much we should be ready to suffer for obedience since for it he who himself is God did not hesitate to die".

Begin by deciding not to believe you are always right, but be willing to take advice from your spouse. If you want to do something one way and your spouse prefers another, do it the way your spouse wants it. Make up your mind not to moan or grumble, but do it "with a will whole, full, and ready" (St Augustine).

There are two contrasting spirits in which you can undertake to be obedient. You can be obedient as a slave is, seeing your spouse's requests as demands which must be followed in order to keep the peace, while you are half-hearted in your service and resentful at the intrusion into your time. The spirit of obedience practiced by free sons and daughters of God, however, is to obey gladly. You do not see it as something you are forced to do, but as something you want to do, because this is where you see yourself really making progress in the Christian life. If you practise obedience in all aspects of your marriage, then, you will slowly become more detached from your own wants and preferences, and you will find something to be happy about in everything that you do.

If you are in a state of obedience to another, never believe your own heart; for it is blinded by its long-standing habitual preoccupations. Do not determine your way of life in anything by your own judgement . . . Do yourself violence in all things and cut off your own will, and, by the grace of Christ living in you, you will become so habituated to cutting off self-will that you do it without constraint or trouble as naturally as you do your own will. Then no longer will you want certain things to happen, but what is happening will be the thing you want and you will be at peace with all.

*St Dorotheus of Gaza*

READINGS FOR FURTHER MEDITATION

Ezekiel 36:25–26
Romans 6:16–19
2 Corinthians 4:5–7
Philippians 2:6–11
Hebrews 5:7–8

# MARRIAGE IS
# A SACRAMENT

# YOU ARE A
# SACRAMENT

The Word was made flesh and dwelt among us.

*John 1:14*

*

*Love made visible*

God loves us and makes Himself known to us through His creation. He is all around us, in the trees, the birds, the animals, the very stones – they all cry out unceasingly, "In Him we live and move and have our being" (Acts 17:28). The world is God's love for us made flesh.

For you it is in your marriage that God's making-flesh of Himself can become most real. Through the faithfulness and the unity you experience in your marriage you can understand something more of the nature of God's eternal love for you. Your marriage can also be a sign of the nature of God for others, as they see it as an open space of loving initiative and response, of healing and the mutual forgiveness of injuries.

God has made His love for you visible: do the same for one another. When you cook a meal, for example, make it an act of love for your spouse. Put your love into the cooking so that the food becomes the means of expressing the love that you have in your heart. Let your love become food, a food that feeds both body and soul.

In showing love, do not despise what seems ordinary or commonplace – every act and every circumstance can be a vehicle for you to express your commitment to your spouse. So constantly look for new and better ways of expressing your love for each other, and your marriage will be a place of God's presence.

## *Love as Christ loves*

Marriage is one of the seven sacraments of the Church. This means that it signifies one of the great mysteries of the Christian faith. The mystery signified by marriage is the covenant of love established by God between human beings and Himself.

You do not signify this mystery as a sign points to something far away: you participate in it. "The word is near you: it is upon your lips and in your heart" (Romans 10:8). And the Lord has brought you into this mystery in order to transform you both in the depths of your hearts so that you can love each other as He loves. Then at last you will be able to say, with St Paul, "the life I now live is not my own life, but the life which Christ lives in me" (Galatians 2:20). The love with which you greet each other then will not be your own love, but the spousal love of Christ. All that God wants of you is that you be completely open to His power working in you both to make this a reality.

## *Become what you are*

You are not a gift to each other only: as a sacrament God has made you His gift to His Church and His world, to be one of the most effective and life-giving signs of His presence. It is not as individuals, but as a married couple, that you are God's sacrament to others. It is in and by your marriage that you are to reveal God.

The sacrament of marriage is not something that you have to earn before you can possess it; nor is it just something that you have in an external sense. As a married couple, joined in the Lord, you *are* a sacrament. Your calling is to "become what you are" – that is, to become in your daily life what, by God's grace, you permanently are in the deepest reality of your marriage. And you are to "become what you are" for others as well as for yourselves. By your very existence you are to be a special sign of God's presence in the world. God trusts married Christians with this vocation, to reveal Him to the world.

## *The Church needs you*

The Church and the world need you to live out your calling as a sacrament. To those who want to see the face of God more clearly the Church has to be able to say, "Come and see" (John 1:39). And it is to you as married people that the Church will point others, for you are supremely the sacrament of God's love and solicitude, the sacrament of His own communion and life.

Sacraments point us to where the Lord can be found, and they reveal His glory. The Gospels tell us that the first place Jesus' glory was revealed was at the marriage in Cana. Here "his disciples saw his glory and they believed in him" (John 2:11). You, too, are to be a place where Jesus reveals His glory, and in this way you will strengthen your fellow Christians in their faith.

Do not, then, be less than you truly are. Do not be content to be simply dutiful, or half-committed, towards one another. The Church needs you to live with each other in the way that

God lives alongside us. She needs you to be a couple who are totally dedicated to each other, completely involved with each other, irrevocably committed to one another's good.

## *His love endures forever*

When you married you made a covenant with each other. This is more than just a contract, which is simply a legal commitment. Making a covenant means that you are personally involved. A contract is only a limited commitment, whereas in marriage you have made a commitment to each other that is unlimited.

Not only marriage, but all of the sacraments of the Church are covenants. They show that God is completely committed to us for our good. In the Scriptures God speaks of Himself as our faithful marriage partner:

> as a young man weds a maiden,
> so shall you wed him who rebuilds you,
> and your God shall rejoice over you
> as a bridegroom rejoices over the bride
>
> *Isaiah 62:5*

God is our Beloved, St Augustine said, and creation is like the ring He has given us as a pledge of His love. Your marriage, then, is a covenant which reflects and shares in the covenantal love God has for all human beings. Your special vocation is to embody this covenant, to allow God to make flesh in your marriage His own marriage to the world.

> Just as of old God encountered his people
> with a covenant of love and fidelity,

78

so our Saviour,
the Spouse of the Church,
now encounters Christian spouses through the sacrament
of marriage.

*Vatican II*

READINGS FOR FURTHER MEDITATION

Isaiah 1:21–26
Isaiah 54:6–7
Jeremiah 3:6–12
Hosea 2:2–17
Matthew 28:20
John 3:29–30
2 Corinthians 11:2
Revelation 19:6–9
Revelation 21:1–3

# THE MYSTERY
# OF MARRIAGE

To you the mystery of the kingdom of God has been given.

*Mark 4:11*

*Reverence*

*

"Sacrament" is the word used to translate St Paul's description of marriage as a "mystery": "Thus it is that (in the words of Scripture) 'a man shall leave his father and mother and shall be joined to his wife, and the two shall become one flesh'. This is a great mystery" (Ephesians 5:31–32).

Your marriage is a mystery because you are both made in the image of God who is eternal Mystery. Just as no systems of thought can ever capture God's essence, so neither reason nor thought on its own can lead you to a final understanding of each other.

It is, of course, important that you try to understand both yourself and your spouse as far as possible, in the complexity of all your feelings and motivations. But if you claim to know each other completely you are in danger of denying one another's uniqueness, as well as the freedom that you both have in Christ to mature and change. Seeing your spouse as a mystery will mean that you recognise that he or she simply does not fit into any neat categories. Your spouse is irreplaceable.

A deep respect for one another should be the foundation of your marriage. All too often, growing familiarity together with the light friction of day-to-day living can mean that spouses treat each other with less than full respect. Always be courteous, then, speaking and acting with great reverence towards one another. Above all, avoid thinking that you know your spouse better than they know themselves. If you have difficulties with your spouse's behaviour, do not imagine that you can read their mind or understand why they are *really* behaving the way they are. Instead, speak about yourself and about your own feelings, and then *ask* them for their reasons for acting as they do – never think that you can tell them.

I hold this to be the highest task of a bond between two people: that each should stand guard over the solitude of the other.

*Rilke*

## True knowledge

There is only one kind of knowledge which reaches into the heart of the mystery of the other person, and that is knowledge that is born out of love.

In God, knowledge and love are inseparable: His knowledge of us is equivalent to His love for us. "Lord, you fathom my heart and you know me", sings the psalmist, "you know where I am, where I go . . . and no word comes to my lips but, my God, you have already heard it" (Psalm 139). The Spirit of God searches the innermost depths of our hearts; He knows us through and through. And the Lord tells us, "I have dearly loved you with an everlasting love, and still I maintain my unfailing care for you" (Jeremiah 31:3). He knows us with His Spirit of love, and He knows us in Christ, who is His love made flesh for us.

This is a deep truth, then, that there is no real knowledge apart from love. Those who claim to know God, or another person, but do not love, are living a lie. Writing about our relationship to God, the author of the *Cloud of Unknowing* said:

> Though we cannot know him we can love him. By love he may be touched and embraced, never by thought.

For you in your marriage it is also the case that the only true knowledge you have of each other will spring from your love for each other. And out of this knowledge-in-love will come new life. Just as "Adam knew Eve his wife and she conceived" (Genesis 4:1), so your marriage will be physically and spiritually fruitful when love becomes your deepest response to the mystery of your spouse.

## Love is the reason

Your loving response to the mystery of your spouse will be incomprehensible to all within you that has not yet been transformed by love. Love cannot be explained in any terms other than itself. Any attempt you might make to give a complete answer as to why you decided to marry each other must flounder on the mystery of love – an answer in terms of a list of qualities you like and admire in your spouse would still leave out what is really essential.

Why do you love each other? "Love is the reason I love", wrote St Bernard. It is because love is the highest reality that nothing else can do justice to it.

> If the supreme reality in God were truth, we should be able to look, with great open eyes into its abysses, blinded

perhaps by so much light, but hampered by nothing in our flight towards truth. But love being the decisive reality, the seraphim cover their faces with their wings, for the mystery of eternal love is such that even the excessive brilliance of its night cannot be glorified except in adoration.

*Hans Urs von Balthasar*

## The heart of the mystery

Marriage is a vocation in which two people undertake to give themselves to one another, and receive themselves back from the hands of the other, transformed by the love and understanding of the other. Two beings of infinite value, you have undertaken to reverence each other with a love and commitment which "pass understanding" (Philippians 4:7). It is a little wonder that St Paul calls marriage – a reality which shares in and mirrors God's own marriage to the world – a *great* mystery!

But this surrender you make to the mystery of the other person will not always be a comfortable experience. It means accepting that you cannot grasp and have each other under your control. And in this lifetime of mutual surrender you are also uncertain which areas of darkness, which hidden depths, in yourself, might suddenly be lighted up. This unveiling of the unknown in ourselves is something we naturally dread because we are never sure how intact it will leave our lives. We want the new life that will come from opening ourselves up to our own depths and to another person, but at the same time we want to stay in control. We want happiness, but only on our own terms.

This is why marriage requires faith. Over and again you will have to make an act of faith that the mystery in yourself and in

83

your spouse to which you have turned yourself over is the mystery of the kingdom of God. When you married you invited God to live within you and between you, so that it would be His Word that you spoke to each other, and His Spirit that united you. Now, just as a mother carries her child within her, your marriage is carried by God, and your life is nourished from His life. You must trust that the Lord is at the heart of the mystery of each of us, and that as you open yourselves more and more to each other so your marriage will be a true sacrament of His presence.

The secret is this: Christ in you, the hope of a glory to come.

*Colossians 1:27*

Men go abroad to wonder at the height of mountains, at the huge waves of the sea, at the vast compass of the oceans, at the long courses of the rivers, at the circular motion of the stars; and they pass by themselves without wondering.

*St Augustine*

READINGS FOR FURTHER MEDITATION

Isaiah 40:12–20
Isaiah 55:8–13
John 123:24–5
Ephesians 1:3–10

# THE PRESENCE
# OF GOD

Keep close to Jesus.

*Abba Paul*

\*

*Christ is entrusted to you*

In order to know better who God is, we want to know where He can be found – where in our lives we can see Him at work, and where we can be close to Him.

In Christ the fullness of God came to dwell among us; He is the sacrament of God, the place where God became flesh so that we could touch even the hem of God's garment and be healed. On the cross Christ poured Himself out, giving birth from His blood and pain to the Church, His bride. She is now the great sacrament of Christ, the new Eve and Mother of all life, continuing the presence of God among us, and she communicates Christ's love and life to all human beings through her sacraments, nourished from "her breasts that give comfort" (Isaiah 66:11).

Christ is a living presence in the sacrament of your marriage, and His presence there binds you even closer to the Church in which is found the completeness of the Lord. Remain close to the Church, then, for "where the Church is, there is the Spirit of God, and where the Spirit of God is, there is the Church and all grace" (St Irenaeus).

85

Just as Christ is the living heart of the Church, so He has promised to be at the heart of your home. God has entrusted Christ to you in your marriage just as He entrusted His Son, as a little child, to Joseph and Mary. Christ is present in the whole of your life together, not just in selected moments. In and through each other He speaks to you, seeks you, calls you to repentance, and loves you.

## Honour Christ in your spouse

The wonderful truth we can proclaim is that God does not keep Himself at a distance. God has visited His people and redeemed them (Luke 1:68). He is the Word of life who has come to make His home with us, so that we can say:

> We have heard it; we have seen it with our own eyes; we looked upon it, and felt it with our own hands; and it is of this we tell ... the eternal life which dwelt with the Father and was made visible to us.
>
> *1 John 1:1–2*

The sacraments give God to us in bodily form. In marriage God comes to you in the bodily form of your spouse. In your husband or wife is Jesus who has promised to be with you always. You made your vows of unending love to each other in fulfilment of this promise of the Lord.

Be sure, then, to take the fact that your marriage is a sacrament with the utmost seriousness. You worship Christ in the sacrament of the altar; Christ is also present in your marriage. Venerate and honour Him in your spouse.

## Discerning the sacrament

> You were there before me, but I had gone away from
> myself and I could not find myself, much less You.
>
> *St Augustine*

God is present in your marriage. But what if you do not
discern Him there? What if you ignore the dignity of your
spouse, taking each other for granted, refusing forgiveness,
being blind to the wonder of their being? Then you bring
judgement upon yourself, for you take the sacrament without
recognising the presence of the Lord (see 1 Corinthians
11:27–32).

The grace of God is always present in your marriage,
whether you are aware of it or not. God is present even when
we ignore or reject Him. But He cannot help you if you are
not open to Him and responsive to Him.

So that the sacrament may be a benefit to you and not a
judgement, take to heart that constant saying of the Lord's to
"keep watch": keep watch over yourself so that you keep a real
reverence for one another in your hearts, and show this
reverence in your words and actions. Take care to be at peace
with one another, and "in one another, honour God, whose
temples you were made to be" (St Augustine).

## Salt of the earth

Christ has called you to be the salt of the earth and the light of
the world (Matthew 5:13–16). This does not simply mean that
you have to be exceptionally good people. If a light is brought
into a room it illuminates what is there. And the purpose of
salt is to preserve and bring out the flavour of the food. Your
task is not primarily to make the world a better place, to create

value – the value is already there. Your task is to show others by your life together how full of wonder and value the world already is. God is already present to you – you do not have to do anything to bring Him into your marriage. Christ is the true Light who will shine out in your marriage and show the glory of your vocation to the world.

God meets us where we are. "In staying still lies your strength" (Isaiah 30:15) because God is with you here and now, whatever the situation, be it good or bad. We have to regain the simplicity to realise this.

## The Spirit is upon you

Your mission is to live out the Good News that God is present with us. The Lord said, "You will bear witness for me in Jerusalem, and all over Judea and Samaria, and away to the ends of the earth" (Acts 1:8).

You are the new Jerusalem, and so when the Lord said that you are to bear witness first in Jerusalem He meant that you should do so first in yourselves and in your marriage. If Christ is not preached to you first, and lived out between you, it will be your own words that you speak and not Christ's gospel; you will be like the prophets condemned by Jeremiah: "there was no word of God in them" (Jeremiah 5:13).

Amma Syncletica said:

> It is dangerous for anyone to teach who has not first been trained in the "practical" life. For if someone who owns a ruined house receives guests there, he does them harm because of the dilapidation of his dwelling. It is the same in the case of someone who has not first built an interior dwelling; he causes loss to those who come.

When you have been obedient to the word preached to you, you are to bear witness in the surrounding districts of Judea and Samaria – that is, to those who are closest to you, your family and friends, your local community and parish. And after that you are to be a witness to all people, wherever you go.

The Spirit has "come upon you with power" (Acts 1:8) so that you can live this vocation to the full. He will give you all you need so that others will say of you, as they said of the first disciples, "see how these Christians love one another".

> Lord, you are in the midst of us
> and we are called by your name.
> Do not forsake us, O Lord our God.
>
> *Jeremiah 14:9*

### READINGS FOR FURTHER MEDITATION

Deuteronomy 30:11–14
Matthew 10:40
Matthew 25:31–46
Luke 24:13–32
John 1:26
John 14:27–28

# A PLACE OF SALVATION

God chose us to possess salvation through our Lord
Jesus Christ

*1 Thessalonians 5:9*

*

### Eucharist for each other

Sacraments are places of meeting. They are not barely
decipherable signs of a God who remains far away, like fingers
pointing into the distance. God comes to us in power in the
sacraments; they are places where salvation is given and
received.

For you who are married it is above all in the sacrament of
your marriage that God is going to effect your salvation. We
are familiar with the general truth that we receive Christ in the
sacraments, but all too often we think only of the Eucharist as
the place of meeting. But for you who are married the
encounter with Christ takes place first of all in your daily
encounter with each other. In your life together *you* are made
eucharist for one another. Daily Christ, who has made you
one with Him in baptism, takes you, gives thanks to the Father
for you, and offers you to your spouse as living bread, as
nourishment for the journey. You have only to consent to this
action of Christ the high priest as He makes you His body,
given in love.

## Midwives

The Lord said, "Unless a man has been born over again he cannot see the kingdom of God" (John 3:3). God delivers us just as a child is "delivered" at birth – salvation is our emergence into a new and wonderful world. This gift of new life is planted like a seed in us at baptism.

Your marriage can be a decisive point in your entry into this new world. There is pain in marriage because your "time has come" (John 16:21) but in the midst of this struggle Christ will give you a foretaste of His joy and peace which no one will be able to take away from you.

The Lord provides us with many aids to encourage and ease our deliverance. He provides us with the sacraments and guidance of the Church, as well as what St Benedict calls "the medicine of divine Scripture". Above all, in your marriage He has given you each other, and called you to be midwives for one another, encouraging the new life to develop, not aborting it for fear of your spouse becoming independent of you. Trust that the emerging life will not threaten your marriage but enrich it all the more.

## That nothing may be lost

God wants to save you together, as two in one flesh. And it is every part of the relationship that He desires to redeem and bring into the kingdom of heaven. "Collect all the pieces", said the Lord, "so that nothing may be lost" (John 6:12). It is all too easy to narrow the idea of redemption so that you imagine that it will include only those parts of yourselves which you consider "spiritual"; but God saves us body and soul together, and we must not call unclean what God has made clean (Acts 10:15).

So do not allow areas in your marriage to fall out of sight because they cause anxiety or are difficult to accept, areas such as sexuality or feelings of anger. Speak and pray together about all aspects of your marriage, entrusting any outcast elements of your lives to the power of Christ so that He is able to integrate these energies into your marriage in a healthy way. Do not be anxious: remember that this process of integration lasts a lifetime. St Augustine prayed,

> In all these dangers and strugglings and others like them,
> You see the shuddering of my heart. I feel not so much
> that I do not suffer from my wounds as that they are
> being healed by You time and time again.

And do not think of salvation as rising above your emotions. The emotions have a vital place in your marriage. Sorrow, fear, desire, compassion, love, delight – all these are essential parts of the spiritual life. To put away emotion would be to put away your humanity. Your redemption is a matter of your being faithful to your hearts' deepest longings, to the vision of loving unity in marriage that has been granted to you.

### Choose to be real

All sin is a matter of choosing to be less than we really are. Sin is choosing to be less than fully real. We sin when we enclose ourselves in the small world of our fantasies and desires because we find this preferable to the world we have actually been given.

You will be tempted to choose unreality whenever life becomes difficult. The appeal of unreality may take many forms: it may be excessive daydreaming; it may be watching television when you know there is something important you need to speak about; or it may be fantasising about some possible future success or love-affair because you feel under-valued at home.

You choose unreality when you try to escape into a private world apart from your bonds of love in marriage, when you turn aside from your marriage commitment and seek a solitary fulfilment. If you do this you are denying your calling, which is to unity, and you are frustrating God's work in your marriage.

Abba Anthony said that without temptations no one could be saved. He knew that we cannot avoid temptations in life, but he saw them as opportunities for making a deeper com-mitment to God's will for us. Place your life together into His hands, then, and let hope make you joyful: "we labour and struggle because we have set our hope on the living God, who is the Saviour of all" (1 Timothy 4:10).

## Bound to one another

> There is no relationship between human beings so close as that of husband and wife, if they are united as they ought to be
>
> *St John Chrysostom*

Your spouse is indeed your "other self", related to the point closest to your heart, as Eve was to Adam. If you are united as you ought to be you will be the image of the unseen God.

If you try to live for yourself in marriage you will break this precious bond; you will lose your life. One early monk said that hell was described to him as a place in which "it is not possible to see anyone face to face, but the face of each one is fixed to the back of another". Hell is the confirmation of the choice to live only for ourselves; it is eternal solitude. Only if, in God, you bind yourselves to one another can you be saved (see Mark 8:35).

Christ died to save us, not from suffering, but from ourselves; not from injustice, far less from justice, but from being unjust. He died that we might live – but live as He lives, by dying as He died who died to Himself.

*George MacDonald*

Come ring out our joy to the Lord,
Hail the God who saves us!
Let us come before him giving thanks,
with songs let us hail the Lord!

A mighty God is the Lord,
a great king above all gods.
In his hands are the depths of the earth,
the heights of the mountains are his.
To him belongs the sea, for he made it,
and the dry land shaped by his hands.

Come in, let us bow and bend low,
let us kneel before the God who saves us,
for he is our God, and we are the people
who belong to his pasture, the flock
that is saved by his hand.

*Psalm 95*

READINGS FOR FURTHER MEDITATION

Psalm 40
Ezekiel 18:21–33
John 16:21–24
Galatians 5:22–25
1 Timothy 2:3–4

# ONE FLESH

Glorify God in your body.

*1 Corinthians 6:20*

\*

*The everlasting marriage*

I will not cease to venerate matter, through which my salvation was brought to pass

*St John of Damascus*

Christianity is a "materialistic" religion. It preaches the holiness of matter. At the centre of our faith stands the Word Who became flesh (John 1:14) – eternal Beauty, eternal Goodness clothed in the vulnerability of flesh, so that He could be touched and seen. Eternal Love was rejected and crucified in the flesh and rose again in the flesh. "Reach your hand here and put it into my side. Be unbelieving no longer, but believe" (John 20:27). If we try to bypass the flesh, not taking it completely seriously, we are unbelievers, avoiding the real scandal of Christ.

But we hate our nakedness, and run away from physical intimacy, hoping to find God even as we hide from one another (see Genesis 3:7): we are afraid of the gift of God appearing in our vulnerability. From the very beginning the major heretics the Church has fought against have been those who were falsely spiritual – who despised earthly happiness,

95

cast doubt on the goodness of the earth, and saw marriage and sexuality as things to be shunned.

When you married you answered God's call to a life of sexual intimacy, proclaiming through your passionate tenderness towards one another that, in Christ, spirit has been joined to flesh in an everlasting marriage. "The things you do in the flesh are spiritual", wrote St Ignatius of Antioch, "for you do all things in union with Jesus Christ".

## Body and soul

To become one flesh is a vocation which involves every aspect of your lives. You cannot become one flesh without the full gift of yourselves to each other. You are called to find in your spouse's happiness your own happiness, to hold their good as your own. Because body and soul are inseparable, your bodily union must be an expression of a union of hearts.

In paradise, said St Thomas, the pleasure that accompanies intercourse would have been even greater because of the immeasurably rich and sensitive love our first parents had for each other. Hold your spouse lovingly in your heart during the day, then, praying for them often, so that your bodily encounter is a celebration of the Christ-given love present in the whole of your marriage.

## A snared beauty

The whole world, including our sexuality, is God's good gift to us. But our inner nature is disordered and no longer understands what goodness truly is but tries to use everything for its own gratification, and our sexuality is drawn into this inner chaos. The world is not a snare: it is we who snare its beauty, perverting it for our own selfish satisfaction. And so

96

the body, which is capable of expressing such loving tenderness, has become prone to selfish excesses. We carry our glory in earthen vessels, said St Paul, and while our lives are disordered, physical sexuality will always conceal this glory even as it tries to bring it to light. Physical passion will always carry a sting of sadness and waste until the Lord has completely healed our wounds.

The manifestation of our inner disorder in sexuality is lust. Lust is a blindness – it is closing your eyes to the wonder of your spouse and focusing your attention upon yourself. Rather than turning outwards to embrace the beloved you simply use them for your own self-seeking. Lust is nothing to do with being carried away by a powerful sexual attraction another has for us – the eyes of the soul are closed to everything but ourselves. This is why St Paul describes those captured by lust as "dead to all feeling" and their hearts "as hard as stone" (Ephesians 4:19).

Guard your heart, then, against both lustful and adulterous desires. When you willingly admit either into your marriage you are unjust to your spouse, because when you married you promised to keep your sexual desires for them alone. If you commit adultery in your heart (Matthew 5:28) you are giving to someone else what belongs to your spouse; and when you are lustful you are like a miser, jealously keeping for yourself what you vowed as a free gift for your beloved.

## Sacrificial love

Our sexuality is central to our lives. And for this reason it is especially marked out for sacrifice, for we must renounce our lives if we would find the true life in Christ. All sacrifices involve the offering up to God of what is good so that it can become the vehicle for what is even better. The genital expression of your affection for one another is a great good, but it always serves the more important good of your union as full persons.

Everything in your marriage must be placed under the control of love, and this includes the expression of your love through genital sexuality. Only if you are able to abstain will your spouse know that sexual intercourse is a free sign of your love. When your spouse is ill, for example, you may show your love partly by abstaining from intercourse. The ability to practice self-control shows that you love your spouse as a whole person and not just their sexuality.

This is also why it is important to respect the natural rhythms of the body rather than use contraceptives. The most fundamental relationship we have, which is to our own bodies, is subverted by substituting artificial control for spiritual control. The redemption of your body means bringing it into a right ordering with the rest of your life, under the power of love.

Abstention will often open up a desert space within you, an affective void in your heart, which you know only the beloved can fill. For it is into the desert that God always calls His people when He wants to renew their love and vision. Make your times of abstention, then, occasions when you show affection in other ways, telling your spouse often how much you love them.

*New life*

A sign of the healthiness of married love is that it generates new life beyond the couple. A central way in which God may grant you this fruitfulness is through the gift of a child. Out of the union of your lives you literally become one flesh in another human person. Because the child *is* the incarnation of your unity, the greatest gift you can give to that child is to grow more deeply in love with each other day by day: then, in your marriage, the child will see and understand that their deepest identity is love.

The fruitfulness God asks of you may take other forms as well, for your unity as a couple is not an end in itself. Every act of love is creative of new life: it may be a hug, a word of encouragement or a meal. Love is fruitful by its very nature. Out of the love of your own marriage, then, turn outwards to serve others, so that you are of use to the Church and the community.

And the two shall become one flesh.

*Mark 10:7*

READINGS FOR FURTHER MEDITATION

Psalm 45
Isaiah 62:2–7
Matthew 5:27–32
1 Corinthians 12:24–26
Titus 1:15

# THREATS TO
UNITY

# ON GUARDING THE HEART AGAINST EVIL THOUGHTS

> I pray thee, not to take them out of the world, but to keep them from the power of the evil one.
>
> *John 17:15*

*

## *Guard your heart*

There are many things with which you will have to struggle in your marriage. Most of all you will have to fight the evil that is within yourself. Jesus told us that evil comes, not from outside of us, but from the heart –

> out of a man's heart come evil thoughts, acts of fornication, of theft, murder, adultery, ruthless greed, and malice; fraud, indecency, envy, slander, arrogance, and folly; these evil things all come from inside, and they defile the man.
>
> *Mark 7:21–3*

In the early church these things that defile us were classified into the "Eight kinds of evil thoughts". They are listed by Cassian and Evagrius as gluttony, impurity, avarice, sadness, anger, acedia, vainglory and pride. The Fathers knew that it was extremely important to recognise these passions and

103

acknowledge their force, because insight into them gives us power over them. And it is through these passions that the devil tries to lead us away from God. Against all these thoughts we must bar the way, and protect the image of God within us. Christ therefore said insistently, "Keep watch"; that is, keep watch over your true self and set up a guard against evil.

You cannot stop these thoughts and desires from coming to you. What matters is how you deal with them.

> A brother came to see Abba Poemen and said to him, "Abba, I have many thoughts and they put me in danger". The old man led him outside and said to him, "Expand your chest and do not breath in". He said, "I cannot do that". Then the old man said to him, "If you cannot do that, no more can you prevent thoughts from arising, but you can resist them".

It is the use we make of the thoughts that matters. Another of the Fathers said that although we can suffer shipwreck through our thoughts, it can be that through courageously resisting them we are crowned.

All real trouble in your relationship will spring from the evil that is within you. To have love and the other virtues in your marriage you must have them first in your heart, for all acts begin in thought. Strive, then, to make yourself free from compulsions, to have a right control over your passions. This is the great work that is given you, patiently cooperating with God as He purifies your heart.

> Put this also to my credit (says Christ) that I preserve you in the desert and put to flight the demons who rage against you.

*Evagrius*

*True security*

Pachomius compared the self to a series of inner chambers. Any weakness, he felt, or any fault lazily accepted, left the whole self exposed, with the enemy in control of some part of us. It is vital to guard against all the suggestions of evil, for the demons use our weaknesses in order to destroy us. Abba Poeman said that the beginning of evil is heedlessness, because the evil spirit, like a shrewd army commander, will attack us at our most vulnerable point. You will only be safe when God is in control of each of the chambers of the self, when He is enthroned as Lord in each part of your heart and in every aspect of your relationship. Pray often, then, showing God your weaknesses and putting your whole trust in Him to protect you.

The devil also uses our pride and false sense of security to attack us. He wants us to rely on ourselves, to deny that we need God. Our greatest moments of weakness are those when we complacently believe ourselves to be strong, to be beyond temptation, when we believe that we have completely mastered our passions. And so St Benedict says, "Place your hope in God alone. If you notice something good in yourself, give credit to God, not to yourself". Your real security lies in humility and trust.

It is said that those who thirst should go to the waters (cf. Isaiah 55:1). Those who thirst for God should go in purity of mind. But he who through such purity soars aloft should also keep an eye on the earth of his own lowliness and simplicity, for no one is more exalted than he who is humble. Just as when light is absent all things are dark and gloomy, so when humility is absent, all our efforts to please God are vain and pointless.

*St Hesychios*

## Discernment

The Fathers give two suggestions for help in controlling our thoughts. The first is discernment. Your disordered inclinations will give rise to many useless thoughts – for example, concerns about false ambitions, or jealousies and unfounded suspicions. You cannot stop thoughts and feelings coming into your mind, but you can learn to discern which are good and helpful and which are bad and distracting. Your task is to discriminate carefully between them, welcoming the good and rejecting the evil. You must learn to be aware of all your thoughts, for unacknowledged thoughts can poison the mind in subtle ways, as they find an entry point in us below our conscious acceptance.

Thoughts are from God if they inspire you to greater confidence in Him; if they strengthen your desire to love both Him and each other more perfectly; if they move you towards greater unity in your married life; and if they help you grow in a healthy self-awareness and at the same time a liberating self-acceptance, knowing that God cares for you just as you are.

Thoughts come from an evil source, however, if they cast you into discouragement and listlessness; if they lead you into fantasy and unreality; if they undermine your faith in God; if they suggest that you are not capable of living the married state as God wants you to; or if they give you a feeling of hopelessness. Most of all the devil wants to lead you to despair, whether it be through awareness of your own sins and failings, or through difficulties in your marriage. The Lord's presence, on the other hand, always gives rise to a fuller life, always leads to wisdom, and eventually gives peace.

*Reveal your thoughts*

The second suggestion the Fathers make concerning the control of thoughts is to reveal them to someone who is walking this same path towards God, who can help us to discriminate between good and evil. Because we are not yet liberated from slavery to our passions, and are often unable to distinguish clearly between what is good and evil, it is helpful to open our inner selves to another person whom we can trust to help us move towards what is good. And so St Benedict says, "As soon as wrongful thoughts come into your heart, dash them against Christ and disclose them to your spiritual father". The power of the thoughts over you is weakened when you reveal them to another person. Cassian writes:

> the devil, subtle as he is, cannot ruin or destroy a junior unless he has enticed him either through pride or through shame to conceal his thoughts. For [the Fathers] lay it down as a universal and clear proof that a thought is from the devil if we are ashamed to disclose it to the senior.

Both monasticism and marriage are paths to God based on an intimate spiritual relationship with another person. For you that person will be your spouse. You share on one another's behalf in God's spiritual fatherhood and motherhood. Freely reveal to each other, then, not only your bad thoughts but whatever occupies your mind. God has given you to each other so that you can help guide each other on the way. Help one another to come to an honest and hopeful self-knowledge. Give your time and energy unsparingly in encouraging one another towards spiritual adulthood. And as far as your own thoughts are concerned, out of reverence for Christ

(Ephesians 5:21), submit yourselves freely to your spouse's judgement concerning their value.

Abba Poeman said of Abba John the Dwarf that he had prayed God to take his passions away from him so that he might become free from care. He went and told an old man this: "I find myself in peace, without an enemy", he said. The old man said to him, "Go, beseech God to stir up warfare so that you may regain the affliction and humility that you used to have, for it is by warfare that the soul makes progress". So he besought God and when warfare came, he no longer prayed that it might be taken away, but said, "Lord, give me strength for the fight".

Drive far from them, O Lord, the spirit
of pride and of vain glory,
of envy and of gloom,
of weariness and slander,
of distrust and despair,
of fornication and uncleanness,
of discord and presumption.
Be in their midst, according to your faithful promise.
And, since you know what each of them needs,
I pray you, strengthen what is weak in them.
Spurn not their frailty, heal that which is diseased,
give joy for sorrow, kindle what is lukewarm,
establish what is insecure in them, that each of them may
know that he does not lack your grace in any of his trials
	and temptations.

*Aelred of Rievaulx*

## READINGS FOR FURTHER MEDITATION

Genesis 8:21
Psalm 3
Jeremiah 6:14
Mark 7:14–23
John 17:14–19
Ephesians 6:10–18

# DOUBT

Where there is no vision the people perish
*Proverbs 29:18*

*

## Trust God's promises

"Love is the kingdom which the Lord mystically promised to the disciples", wrote Isaac the Syrian. "When we have reached love, we have reached God and our journey is complete. We have crossed over to the island that lies beyond the world, where are the Father, the Son and the Holy Spirit". This is the land the Lord has prepared for you, your journey's end, a place of "rest", the land for which you were created.

St Paul tells us that God had prepared this place of rest for the Israelites, so that they had only to step into it and enjoy the good things there, but they would not. There was no barrier, but they erected one out of their own doubts and fears. They did not trust that God really had their good at heart and that He wanted to give them this land. "It was their unbelief which prevented their entering" (Hebrews 3:19). They doubted both God's willingness to protect them and His power to do so – perhaps He had brought them into the desert to die? Perhaps His hand was not so strong?

If you want to enter the kingdom of love, then, you must abandon yourselves entirely to God. Remember that the Father wants to give you this Kingdom (see Luke 12:32) – He does not want to keep you out. He has given you so much already: trust Him to give you what your hearts most desire. Do not doubt God's ability to work in you and your marriage, or you will never enter the land of perfect love. Believe rather that, "He knows all, He can do all, and He loves us".

## You do not believe

The Lord has told us that He loves us unconditionally, that He died to redeem us, and that we are worth everything to Him. God has revealed Himself to us as our lover. "I have told you", says the Lord, "but you do not believe" (John 10:25).

We find it so hard to believe. For you who are married, then, God has sent another sign of His love to you: He has given you each other to be a living expression of His total commitment to you. You have before you a person who has given the whole of their life to you, a sure sign to you of your worth.

Yet we continue to hear the doubting voice of Satan instead. He is the "accuser of the brethren" (Revelation 12:10), who accuses them day and night, telling them that they are worth nothing. His aim is to bring you to despair of God, of yourself and of one another, because only then can he have power over you. And so he will tempt you to sin, to make you despair of yourself when you find that you do not live up to your ideals; he will suggest to you that maybe your spouse thinks they made a mistake in marrying you. He will tell you that they have seen through you now and see you for what you really are – immature, childish, full of weaknesses and faults. The father of lies (John 8:44) will tell you that no one could love you when they really know you.

Then you will draw back from offering yourself to each

other and begin to *do* things for each other instead, trying to prove your value through your gifts. You will begin to be insecure and jealous. Finally you will manage to turn everything they say and do into a living confirmation of what you see as the fact that you are worthless.

The devil is a liar and you must utterly reject his suggestions. Cry out with the psalmist, "save me from lying lips" (Psalm 120:2), and say to the Lord, "thy word is founded on truth" (Psalm 119:160). You can rely on the Lord's word, for He is truth itself and no darkness or lies are to be found in Him. Your true worth is the worth which He finds in you, for He is the only reality. Rejoice in this, then, and believe your spouse when they tell you they love you, for they have seen you as God sees you.

## *Live the vision*

When you first married you had a marvellously clear vision of the value of your spouse and of the importance of your vocation. You gave yourself to it gladly, certain of what you were doing. So do not now allow the passing of time to cast a veil over what you have seen with such clarity. You have been granted a vision of great beauty, as the glory of the Lord overshadowed you both and revealed to each of you the other's eternal splendour. Under the power of that vision you were able to love almost without effort. Now you have the task of growing, day by day, into a person of stable character who lives by the truth of this vision.

Sometimes you may find that doubts about the importance of marriage or the value of your spouse will be awakened in you because you meet with a lack of understanding in others. They may ask you why you want to spend so much time together, why you value unity so highly, or why you do not

112

place your career above your marriage. Hold fast to the truth that has been revealed to you (see 1 John 1:1–2) and remember that only the eyes of love can truly see the value that is present.

At other times the sheer ordinariness of married life may cause you to lose sight of the splendour to which your marriage is called. But none of us should deserve the rebuke of the Lord that "You have lost your early love" (Revelation 2:4). We have seen the land of eternal love through, as it were, a door held ajar for a short moment. Now let us joyfully walk the road to that land.

## *Walking on the water*

For all Christians, life is a continual walking on the water. We have to follow Peter who was called by the Lord out of the safety of the boat. He was able to walk across the sea towards Jesus supported by the rock of faith that was invisible to the eye. Peter began to drown only when he took his eyes off the Lord and looked instead at the waves around him, breaking over his feet.

So also the devil prowls around like a roaring lion, seeking to devour you, but has no power over you unless you doubt that God is able to help. It is only through fear that the lion is able to catch his prey. But when you are afraid you grow irritable, worrying over things and putting unnecessary pressure on each other; you demand assurances of love and will not believe them when they are given to you! Therefore St Peter says, "Stand up to him, strong in faith" (1 Peter 5:8) and St James reassures us, "Stand up to the devil and he will turn and run" (James 4:7).

Evil has no power and no reality. In order to tempt Job, Satan had first to ask permission from God (Job 1:2), just as the demons had to ask Jesus' permission to enter the pigs: this shows clearly that everything that happens comes under the providence of God. This is why St Anthony, who underwent many trials sent by the devil, only became all the more fearless in his fight. He treated the forces of hell with contempt because he trusted totally in God's power to defeat them. The demons are weak, he said, and can do nothing except threaten, and so we should despise them and fear only God. So do not be afraid, and do not doubt. The Lord said, "I am with you always, to the end of time" (Matthew 28:20).

> Jesus said: "I tell you this: if you have faith no bigger even than a mustard-seed, you will say to this mountain, 'move from here to there!', and it will move; nothing will prove impossible for you".
>
> *Matthew 17:20*

READINGS FOR FURTHER MEDITATION

Psalm 23
Psalm 95
Luke 10:19
Hebrews 3:15 – 4:1
Revelation 12

# ANGER

The deadly poison of anger has to be totally rooted out
from the inmost corners of our soul.

*Cassian*

\*

## The purpose of anger

It is part of being human to feel angry, just as it is human to
feel hurt, jealous or excited. The feeling of anger is not good
or bad in itself. You do not choose to have it; it simply comes.
It is what you do with anger that is important. It need not be a
threat to your love for each other. Anger may be revealing
where there is a problem in your married life and in this way
illuminating an area where a closer union can be formed
through increased knowledge and acceptance of one another.
It is an opportunity for further growth into one flesh.

There is also a positive purpose for which anger has been
given to us by God – it is a powerful energy to use against evil.
St Isaiah the Solitary wrote, "Without anger a man cannot
attain purity: he has to feel angry with all that is sown in him
by the enemy". Direct your anger, then, against your own sin,
for sin is alien to your true self.

What the Fathers oppose with all their might, however, is
anger that is nursed in the heart, anger that is used to put
others down, anger that issues in words and actions that
wound your spouse. It is in this sense that Christ commands
you to root out anger from your inmost selves (Matthew 5:22),

115

and St Paul tells you to put away all anger since it grieves God's Spirit (Ephesians 4:30–31). Dorotheos of Gaza wrote that "It is impossible for a man to be angry with anyone unless his heart is first lifted against him, unless he despises him and esteems himself superior to him". Therefore, as long as you hold anger in your hearts God's Spirit cannot dwell in your marriage.

## Anger comes from within

St John of the Cross wrote,

> It is not the will of God that the soul allow aught to trouble it, or suffer trials; if it suffer them in the adversities of the world, this comes from the weakness of its virtue; for the soul of the perfect man rejoices in that which causes the imperfect soul affliction.

We tend to think of anger as something which is brought into us from outside by difficult events. Things people do to us and say to us *make* us angry. We were not angry before we saw the mess on the floor, but seeing this put anger inside us. But Christ said clearly that anger lies on the heart, as do all the vices, and that events from outside merely awaken what is already within. Other people, their actions and words, simply bring out the passion that is within us. We are not made angry; we *are* angry.

Because we think of anger as an external reality we think that we are fully justified in responding with indignation when we feel this way; we think that all our anger can be called "righteous anger"; we think that it is the other person who is at fault. And so we say that they must be made to see the error of their ways. It is the other person who must change, not us. Listen to what Dorotheos of Gaza says about this:

116

Again there is the case of a man minding his own business, sitting at peace and quiet; and when a brother comes up and says an annoying word to him, he is put out by it. And from the circumstances he thinks that he is justifiably angered, and he speaks against the one who troubled him, saying, "If he had not come and spoken to me and annoyed me I should not have been at fault." This is a delusion; this is false reasoning! For it was not the one who spoke who put him in a bad mood. He only showed that it already existed in him; so that he could, if he chose, make reparation for his fault. But the man referred to above is like clean-looking winter wheat, externally good and ready to use; but when someone crushes it, its corruption is revealed. He was sitting at peace, as we were saying, but he had this anger inside him and he did not know it.

Your anger, then, is a call for both of you to change and to grow in self-knowledge. Feelings of anger are often a defence, covering up our hurts and frustration, so that an apparently small occasion or insignificant remark may open up a great void of fear within us. Ask yourself why you felt so angry in the situation – after all, not everyone would have reacted with anger as you did. And the Fathers knew well that we are often angriest with what we hate most in ourselves.

## Seeking a false peace

Much of our anger springs from self-will: life is not as we want it and people are different from us and do not do things the way we would do them. And so even if we lived among angels, St John of the Cross says, some things would seem wrong to us. In its fallen condition the soul seeks a false peace,

117

which is that of having everything organized just as it would have it. And since this is impossible the soul is never at peace. And so we are not only angry with other human beings but with inanimate objects as well – we are angry with the car when it stalls, with the weather for being too hot or too cold, and with our pen for running out. The answer is not to avoid what angers us, for anger is within and will emerge wherever we are and whatever we do. If we are angry within we will always find something to annoy us.

"Sometimes", writes Cassian, "when we have been overcome by pride or impatience, and we want to improve our rough and bearish manners, we complain that we require solitude, as if we should find the virtue of patience there where nobody provokes us: and we apologise for our carelessness, and say that the reason for our disturbance does not spring from our own impatience, but from the fault of our brethren." But laying the blame on other people, he says, is not the answer. Rather, "the fact that we are not angry ought not to result from another's perfection, but from our own virtue, which is acquired, not by somebody else's patience, but by our own long-suffering".

## The right measurements

To judge clearly we must be able to see clearly. But because our hearts are still crooked, and because we have only our own partial perspective, we make false judgements when we set ourselves up as the standard of what is right and wrong, and when we make our attitudes the standard of what is "normal" and "reasonable". We may just happen to have a fetish for order, and hate to see anything out of place, or we may be workaholics and feel that any form of relaxation is laziness. And so the Lord said,

118

Why do you look at the speck of sawdust in your brother's eye, with never a thought for the great plank in your own? Or how can you say to your brother, "Let me take the speck out of your eye", when all the time there is that plank in your own?

*Matthew 7:3–4*

Because of the plank in our eye our anger lacks proportion; we lose sight of the other person and their action and see only how we are affected.

Only God's measurements are true. If you accept that you are an unsound measuring rod for what is acceptable and unacceptable you will go some way towards conquering your anger. Reject anger, then, for it "blinds with hurtful darkness the eye of the soul", and while we remain angry "we can neither acquire right judgement and discretion, nor gain the insight which springs from an honest gaze" (Cassian). Put in love instead, for love alone sees clearly.

## Dealing with anger

The Fathers suggest two more ways of dealing with anger. The first, and most important, is communication. For your marriage to mature you must share the full range of your feelings with your spouse, and not just the sweet ones. Explain how you feel when the soap is left swimming in a pool of water in the soap dish, or when your loving overtures are ignored – your spouse will be able to show their love for you by trying to alter their behaviour on this point. It will help if you realise that not everybody would have felt angry at this: you are a unique person and your reaction tells you as much about yourself as about your spouse.

Expressing your feelings is one thing, having a violent

outburst is quite another: do not be aggressive towards your spouse. But do not try to hide your anger: if it is not expressed it will slowly poison your relationship – you will act out your anger through depression, silence, or distancing yourself from your spouse. The most important thing is to overcome the problem together. In this way, even anger will be the occasion for a deeper unity between you.

The second thing the Fathers advise is to trust God completely, knowing that He has care of you both and that nothing can happen apart from His providence. You are often angry when you feel that your needs have not been met. Even then, however, do not be angry, but remember that your Heavenly Father knows what you need (Matthew 6:32). Pray together about what occasions anger, asking the Lord to lead you both towards greater reliance on Him.

> Don't you see that this is why we make no progress, why we find we have not been helped towards it? We remain all the time against one another, grinding one another down. Because each considers himself right and excuses himself . . . all the while keeping none of the Commandments yet expecting his neighbour to keep the lot!
>
> *Dorotheos of Gaza*

READINGS FOR FURTHER MEDITATION

Proverbs 27:4–6
Matthew 5:21–26
2 Corinthians 5:16–21
Ephesians 4:30–31

# DISCOURAGEMENT

The Lord is near; have no anxiety.
*Philippians 4:6*

\*

## Rejoice without ceasing

Discouragement can be a great affliction in the Christian life. It is more than disappointment, and more than just the sadness that can come from being very tired. It is a real despondency, leading us to think about giving up all our efforts and good intentions. We become dejected, the future seems to hold nothing in store for us, and we feel that we are not really getting anywhere. We begin to neglect our vocation, we try to get away with doing as little as possible, and we do not even care that we are putting in so little effort. It is a terrible temptation to listen to voices like this inside us, for they can get great power over us.

The Fathers remind us that in some sense the origin of dejection is within us – there is some basic disorder or disease in our hearts which external circumstances have brought out. We are sad and weary of life because we are wounded in the very depths of our being, because we are cut off from God who is the source of all life and all that is really good for us. The immediate occasion of discouragement, which reveals this disorder, may be tiredness or anxiety about some problem, it may be a disappointment, or it may be depression about our faults. Whatever the source, it is vital that together, you resist the spirit of discouragement in your marriage. Abba Apollo used to say, "Those who are going to inherit the kingdom of heaven must not be despondent about their salvation". Those who are occupied with earthly things, he said, "rejoice in their earthly concerns, but we who have been considered worthy of so great a hope, how shall we not rejoice without ceasing?"

## Tiredness

> Some old men came to see Abba Poemen and said to him, "When we see brothers who are dozing at the synaxis, should we rouse them so that they will be watchful?" He said to them, "For my part when I see a brother who is dozing, I put his head on my knees and let him rest".

Depression can come simply from tiredness: overwork and sheer physical exhaustion can lead to despondency as we feel harassed or resentful that we are being asked to do so much. St Benedict understood this and addressed this problem several times in his Rule. He quotes Jacob who said, "If I drive my flocks too hard, they will all die in a single day" (Genesis 33:13). Everything, therefore, must be done in moderation. Too much activity, apart from tiring us, can take us from our primary vocation, which is to love and to contemplate. It has been said that if you are too busy to pray, then you are too busy. And the same applies to time to relax and talk together in your marriage – if you do not have time for this you are also too busy.

St Benedict said that work should be divided according to different people's strength. Help one another, then, so that you carry the necessary work together and both avoid over-work and exhaustion. "Help one another to carry these heavy loads, and in this way you will fulfil the law of Christ" (Galatians 6:2).

## God has made me laugh

Discouragement can come from difficulties we have with our own temperament: we can feel at times that we will never be able to overcome some particular fault in ourselves. At this point our thoughts can suggest to us that we give up, that we are only mediocre people anyway and not really capable of living the Christian life. We are overcome with sorrow and depression and give up all thought of reforming ourselves, slowly ceasing to pray or practice our faith in any way.

Let your sorrow at your own sins lead you rather to seek amendment of your lives. It is true that we cannot live the Christian life on our own, it is true that it is beyond our strength to do so. But we are never alone. And therefore St Benedict says, "What is not possible to us by nature, let us ask the Lord to supply by the help of his grace". Christians are people who set off on their journey certain that they can reach their destination. Their trust is not in their own power, but in the power of God. This trust will help you to rise again after falling without losing a single moment; it will help you to leave the past behind, looking forward to the new day as a day in which God will be with you to fight against your weaknesses. Listen to these wonderful words of St John of Karpathos:

> To anyone among you who is oppressed by a sense of his worthlessness and inability to attain holiness, this is our message: . . . Though his soul, like Sarah, has grown old in barrenness, it can still bear a holy child, contrary to all

expectation; like her he can still say: "God has made me laugh" (Genesis 21:6) – that is, God has granted me great joy after the many years that I have spent in sorrow, dominated by the passions.

## The demon of Exaggeration

Great sadness can also come from painful situations, from problems which take a long time to resolve, or from disappointments. It normally attacks you at moments when you had expected happiness, but do not get what you had hoped for. The demon of Exaggeration then uses this small incident to overwhelm you with sadness. Perhaps you were hoping to make love and your spouse is too tired: the demon uses this to suggest to you that they are always too tired, that they have never enjoyed love-making as much as you have, and that it will probably be a long time in the future before they will want to make love again. The demon goes on to suggest to you that your spouse always looks tired now and conjures up before your eyes a lengthy old age without intercourse. The power of this demon lies in its ability to lead you to reflect on isolated moments of disappointment until it has undermined and cast doubts on the whole of your life.

When our desires are not met, and we cannot have what we want, our thoughts often lead us on to day-dream about our lives, and "when these thoughts find that the soul offers no resistance but rather follows after them and pours itself out in pleasures that are still only mental in nature, they then seize her and drench her in sadness, with the result that these ideas she was just indulging no longer remain. In fact they cannot be had in reality, either ... So the miserable soul is now shrivelled up in her humiliation to the degree that she poured herself out upon these thoughts of hers" (Evagrius). Disappointment, then, can lead us to try to find a false fulfilment of desire in the mind alone when it has been denied us in reality. Firmly resist this fantasising, which leads only to spiritual death. The place where God will meet you is in your marriage and your life as it is.

## Changing feelings

Sometimes we just feel down in the dumps. Perhaps you miss being with your wider family at Christmas, or with a friend of whom you used to see much before you were married. Or perhaps it is just a change in the weather or a vague feeling that life seems a bit empty. Whatever the reason, be ready to encourage each other, and be available to listen if your spouse wants to talk. St Paul tells us to put heart into each other for fear that sorrow overwhelm us at any time (see 2 Corinthians 2:5–8). Remember that life is bound to feel like this some-times, which is why St Benedict tells the new monk not to be daunted by fear and run away when things seem hard. These feelings pass, and if you keep your eyes fixed on God and on His great love for you these occasions will be a time for you to strengthen your commitment to God and to one another.

> If I lift up my eyes to the hills,
> where shall I find help?
> Help comes only from the Lord,
> maker of heaven and earth.
> How could he let your foot stumble?
> How could he, your guardian, sleep?
> The guardian of Israel never slumbers, never sleeps.
> *Psalm 121:1–4*

## *Encouragement*

Do not look forward to the changes and chances of this life in fear; rather look to them with full hope that as they arise, God – whose own you are – will deliver you out of them. He has kept you hitherto, do you but hold fast to His dear hand and He will lead you safely through all things; and when you cannot stand He will bear you safely in His arms. What need you fear, my child, remembering that you are God's and that He has said, "All things work together for good to those who love Him". Do not look forward to what may happen tomorrow. The same everlasting Father who cares for you today will take care of you tomorrow and every day. Either He will shield you from suffering or He will give you unfailing strength to bear it. Be at peace then. Put aside all anxious thoughts and imaginations and say continually, "The Lord is my strength and my shield, my heart has trusted in Him and I am helped; He is not only with me but in me and I in him."

What can a child fear surrounded by such a Father's arms?

*St Francis de Sales*

READINGS FOR FURTHER MEDITATION

Psalm 77
Psalm 121
Luke 11:5–13
1 Thessalonians 5:16–18

# THE DESIRE TO DOMINATE

All men desire to be at peace with their own people, while desiring to impose their will upon those people's lives

*St Augustine*

*

## *The brightest jewel*

Rather than allowing God to remake us in His image, all too often we try to remake those with whom we live in *our* image. We try to be their only source of life. We want them to live in dependence on us, to live under our influence. And if they try to find life elsewhere then we subtly take our revenge – by our reserve, our coldness or by some kind of emotional blackmail. We insist on being the centre of their lives.

In all communities there is a strong temptation to live like this, and perhaps most of all in the community of marriage. It results in the sad state of affairs where husband and wife only really feel free to be themselves when they are apart from each other, or have the support of others, because both feel dominated by the other.

We cannot, of course, be the only source of life and goodness for others. Our attempts to be this must fail. We are like the man who tried to build his house on sand (Matthew

7:26–7): it will always be washed away. Be glad when these illusions are stripped from you, even though it is often very painful. We must die to ourselves for new life to grow, and this new life can only come into your marriage when all such pride is removed. Be glad, then, even when you are ignored or passed-over. Make these times opportunities for understanding that your brightest jewel is really your poverty of spirit, your need for God. This is the way to lasting peace in your own heart, and between both of you in your marriage.

## Humility

The desire to dominate will manifest itself in the attempts you make to control one another's lives. You will want to monitor who your spouse meets and what they read, where they go and how they look (all this for their own good, of course!).

The desire to dominate is characterised by envy and suspicion. If you give in to it, therefore, you will find yourselves restlessly curious about everything and everyone. It feeds on harsh judgements, since it is always looking for shortcomings in others so that it can rejoice in its own superiority. In fact, it has to deny the existence of anything of real interest or goodness outside of itself so that it can remain the only focus of attention.

Only Christ can save us from pride. He is good precisely because He does not care about His own glory (John 8:50). "Why do you call me good?", He asks; "No one is good except God alone" (Mark 10:18). His divinity shines out above all in his humility, in His recognition that everything is a gift from the Father. St Paul tells us to imitate Christ in His humility when he says,

There is nothing for anyone to boast of. For we are

128

God's handiwork, created in Christ Jesus to devote ourselves to the good deeds for which God has designed us

*Ephesians 2:9–10*

## Ruled by each other

How beautiful it is that the second human being was
taken from the side of the first, so that nature might teach
that human beings are equal and, as it were, collateral,
and that there is in human affairs neither a superior or an
inferior, a characteristic of true friendship.

*Aelred of Rievaulx*

Married love is the highest form of friendship, because in
marriage there is equality together with a wonderful degree of
intimacy. St Paul described the equality that there should be
in a Christian marriage in this way:

the wife does not rule over her own body, but the
husband does; likewise the husband does not rule over
his own body, but the wife does

*1 Corinthians 7:4*

Equality in marriage is not a matter of having equal rights.
It is something quite different: a state in which there is an
equal giving-over of yourselves to be ruled by one another,
and equal service. The husband gives himself wholly to be
ruled by his wife; the wife, likewise, submits in all things to her
husband. In this way, marriage becomes a glorious revelation
of the Trinity, of the mutual bestowing of glory among the
divine Persons. Be subject to each other, then, out of reverence for Christ (Ephesians 5:21).

129

E

## Fear

The desire to dominate has its deepest roots in fear. Because we fear that what is most important to us will be taken away we grasp it tightly to ourselves, and in doing so we choke the life from it. Fear was the real origin of Adam's fall, and is therefore the deepest wound in our being. God had made Adam and Eve in His own image, creating them for immortality (Wisdom 2:23). But they doubted His promise and wondered, "does God really desire our good?" Because they would not trust God, they tried to steal their security from Him. They fell when they tried to take from God what God was, in fact, freely offering them. They wanted to possess as a right what could only be continually received as a free gift.

In your marriage, if you try to take love you will destroy it at its roots. Be more concerned to give than to receive. Above all, give freedom. Help your spouse to escape from your influence, and rejoice to see God moulding them into the unique and wonderful creature He desires them to be.

Let there be no jealousy between you concerning your different gifts and virtues. "How rare a virtue it is", said St Bernard to his monks, "not to envy the virtue of another, not to mention rejoicing in it". The ideal for which you should aim is well expressed by St Gregory Nazianzen who spoke of his friendship with St Basil in these terms: "There was indeed a combat between us. But it was not as to who should have the first place for himself but how he could yield it to the other. For each of us regarded the achievement of the other as his own."

## Freedom

You will be able to give freedom to each other only when you yourself have found freedom in the love God has for you. When God is the centre of your life you will want Him to be the centre of your marriage also.

The centre of the Lord's life was God the Father: He wanted no name for Himself except "the Son", in order to show that the entire meaning of His existence lay in His relationship with His Father. Likewise, St Paul said that his true life lay "hidden with Christ in God" (Colossians 3:3). In the Trinity the centre is nowhere, for none of the Persons seeks to make themselves centre. The unity in God is to be found in the mutual self-giving of the Persons each for the Other. Let this be the pattern for your marriage as you strive to outdo each other in showing love.

Love is their guide as they eat, as they talk, in their conduct, in their demeanor. They are united in one love, and that love is the air they breathe. What injures that love is seen as an offence against God. What is hostile to love will be fought, will be rejected; what does harm to love must be suppressed that very day. For they well know that Christ and His Apostles teach that everything is vain if love alone is lacking, but that all is made perfect if love is present

*St Augustine*

READINGS FOR FURTHER MEDITATION

John 8:48–58
John 17:4–5
1 Corinthians 7:3–4
Philippians 2:1–4

# LIVING TOGETHER

# LIVING SIMPLY

In simplicity of heart I have gladly offered everything.
*1 Chronicles 29:17*

\*

## One will

St Bernard said that simplicity is the radiance of the soul. It is the treasure hidden in the field for which we must dig and work. Although we are naturally simple of heart he said that we have become unnatural and live in dividedness and duplicity instead. We live in a state of inner conflict, of conflict with each other and of conflict with God because we have lost our simplicity. To be simple means to return to a state of unity, harmony and order. We will have regained our simplicity when our will is one with God's will, because His order is the only real order.

In marriage you can regain your simplicity. You have each given yourselves wholly to one person, making them your priority. Keep your gaze simple and uncluttered, then, focused in love upon your spouse, living with an undivided heart. If you seek this one thing that is necessary (Luke 10:42) you will make of your two wills one single will in God. Then, as St Augustine said, you will be "together one, in the one Christ, on the way to the one Father".

## Offer everything

You can come to simplicity only through the destruction of self-will. It is self-will which makes you seek your own good at the expense of your spouse, which encourages you to put yourself first, not thinking what is best for your marriage. It is self-will which makes you prefer career, or relaxation, or some other pastime to the love of your husband or wife.

David said: "In simplicity of heart I have gladly offered everything" (1 Chronicles 29:17). Let that be your goal: to offer everything, to hold back nothing for yourself. "Nothing is more glorious", said Richard of St Victor, "than to wish to have nothing that you do not share". If you live like this your marriage will be a living image of God, for His very being is eternal self-gift.

Offer everything, then, and make of yourselves living sacrifices: this is the worship which pleases God the Father (Romans 12:1). And do not think that you are giving little when you give yourselves: you are the pearl of great price for whom the Lord sold all that He had that He might gain you (Matthew 13:45–46). Your spouse, too, has given all, forsaking all others, because they have seen your value.

## Simple in speech

Teach your mouth to say that which you have in your heart

*Abba Poeman*

Simplicity means openness with each other, it means speaking without hidden meanings, without sarcasm or cynicism. The root of duplicity is a lack of trust: we fear to speak simply and to give ourselves fully to each other in case we are misunderstood, or are not accepted. Simplicity, therefore, is the responsibility of the one who listens as much as the one who speaks. Your marriage can only enter the kingdom of heaven if you become as simple as children with each other (Matthew 18:3).

All sincere and open sharing of yourselves involves uncovering your nakedness, which since the Fall we have seen as something shameful. "I was afraid because I was naked", we say to one another, "and so I hid myself" (Genesis 3:10). But to those who hide themselves in fear, who do not let themselves be known, who cover themselves in the cloak of deceit, God must say at the last, "I never knew you" (Matthew 7:23).

It is love which casts out this fear perfectly. Therefore beg the Holy Spirit to pour His love into your marriage, as well as His wisdom and understanding, so that what is covered in fear in both of you may be gradually uncovered, and your simplicity shine out.

> Nothing is loved except by being understood,
> nor understood except by being loved
> *William of St Thierry*

## Possessions

Let your lifestyle be simple. This means having a right order in your priorities. The Lord taught us that serving God and money are mutually exclusive: "No one can serve two masters", He said, "you cannot serve God and mammon" (Luke 16:13). You serve God rather than mammon when the practice of virtue is more important to you than the number and quality of your possessions. You are serving God rather than mammon when your attention and desires are focused on each other rather than on the things you possess.

137

In this way you will teach your children by your own example that the true treasures are the treasures of the heart, inner riches which cannot be bought or sold. Do not be like those of whom St Cyprian says: "You who are more careful about your children's earthly estate than their heavenly, commending them rather to the devil than to Christ, are twice sinful! You deny them the aid of God their Father and you teach them to love property more than Christ". Set your minds firmly on the values of God's kingdom, confident that He will make sure that you have all you need.

Never covet what others have, for "possessions are so called that we may possess them, not they possess us" (St John Chrysostom). Find your freedom of spirit in being content with what you have, and use your possessions to help any who are in need, especially through generous hospitality.

## A place of simplicity

God breathes His Spirit into all creation, and so everything we see and touch is holy. It was for this reason that St Benedict insisted that all the goods of the monastery were to be handled with the same care and respect as the sacred vessels of the altar. So, too, every part of your home is a holy place. Be aware that the sanctifying Spirit, who fills the whole universe, makes your home – for you and for all who enter it – a gateway to heaven, a stairway to God. The Lord has promised you: "this is my resting place for ever; here will I make my home, for such is my desire" (Psalm 132:14). Let it be, then, a place of simplicity and beauty, a reflection of God who is Simplicity and Beauty itself.

Some day we must attain to the same love God has for us. We must reach the point where, just as God wills all things to exist only for himself, so we too may will to have existed and to exist, and will everything else to have been or to be solely for the sake of God and on account of his will alone, not for our own pleasure. We shall then delight, not in the fact that all our needs have been satisfied . . . but in the fact that his will in us and for us will then be seen to be completely accomplished and carried out.

*St Bernard of Clairvaux*

READINGS FOR FURTHER MEDITATION

1 Chronicles 29:10–19
Psalm 23
Tobias 4:5–11
Matthew 6:25–34

# HOSPITALITY

Let all guests be received as though they were Christ, for
he will say, "I was a stranger and you took me in".

*Rule of St Benedict*

*

## Pilgrims together

We can learn from Scripture the importance of hospitality in
our lives, especially from Abraham, our father in faith.
Because of his hospitality he entertained angels without knowing it. Although he had hundreds of servants, when the three
visitors arrived he personally served his guests, making sure
that all their needs were met. For his guests he himself became
a servant, just as Christ came not to be served but to serve.

Give hospitality to all. You have a special duty to care for
members of your own family, from whom you have already
received much. Remember other Christians as well, members
with you in the family of faith. You are pilgrims together
seeking the heavenly country. Make particularly welcome
those without families of their own, and those who are far
from home – the lonely, old people without children or whose
children live far away, those forced to work far from home.
You may also be called to the hospitality of fostering or
adopting children. Offer hospitality freely and willingly, then,
without grudging, for God loves a cheerful giver. It is better to
give than to receive.

## Receiving the Lord

By offering hospitality we receive Christ into our homes. In the guest it is Christ who says,

> Behold, I stand at the door and knock: if anyone hears my voice and opens the door, I will come in and sit down to supper with him and he with me
>
> *Revelation 3:20*

Open the doors of your hearts, then, as well as the door of your home, because it is Christ you see in your brother or sister, it is Christ you feed at your table.

In the poor, whether spiritually, emotionally or materially, Christ is especially to be received. In them you see the Son of Man who has nowhere to lay His head, the Word of God who seeks shelter and rest in your home. In the guest, whether family or stranger, rich or poor, we encounter the Lord who comes under our roof even though we are not worthy to receive Him.

## The hospitality of God

We are able to offer hospitality because we have experienced the hospitality of God. We love because He first loved us. At baptism we were welcomed into God's household, and since then God's love and forgiveness have been lavished upon us whenever we have returned home poor and in distress at our own sins.

Take every opportunity to accept God's invitation to feast at His table. In the eucharist Christ Himself is the divine host who receives us, and whom we receive into ourselves as He feeds us with the bread and wine of immortality, His Body and

Blood. In the eucharist, the Word becomes flesh and dwells within us and we become homes of the Spirit of God. And so Abba James says, "It is better to receive hospitality than to give it".

We are being truly hospitable when we offer God's hospitality to others. By opening ourselves up more to God, by allowing Him to come to make His home in us, we are also enabled to give more to others. The quality of our hospitality, then, depends upon our constancy in prayer and worship. If we have not received Christ we will have nothing to give to others except our own emptiness. Jesus says to us,

> Dwell in me, as I in you. No branch can bear fruit by itself, but only if it remains united with the vine; no more can you bear fruit, unless you remain united with me
>
> *John 15:4*

In order to care for others as we should, in the way they need, we have to have allowed God into our lives to care for us.

> May you learn to spill over only from fulness and not want to be more generous than God ... First be filled, and then spill over under supervision. Kind and prudent love does not flow outwards until it abounds within.
>
> *St Bernard of Clairvaux*

## An inclusive marriage

A brother came to see a certain hermit and, as he was leaving, he said, "Forgive me, abba, for preventing you from keeping your rule". The hermit replied, "My rule is to welcome you with hospitality and to send you away in peace".

Have a simple, open attitude towards others, and let your marriage be inclusive rather than closed in on itself. Reach out gladly to include others in your married and family life. Otherwise you may be like Dives, who feasted every day on the riches of his house, but failed to notice Lazarus at his gate. Hospitality is one of the key marks of a Christian household.

At the same time, remember that your marriage is a relationship that needs its own special attention. So the Lord says regularly to you, as a married couple, "Come away with me by yourselves. Close the door and speak to each other in secret". Just as monastic rules provide for the necessary separation of guests from the permanent household, so you must take care that time is given to your spouse and family. The quality of your hospitality will depend upon the quality of your family relationships.

Be natural and relaxed with your guests, caring but not fussily-caring. Do not be too concerned about how tidy your home is, or how elaborate the meals you offer. Love is more important than food and approachability more than a neat and orderly home. Both Martha and Mary received Christ, however, and good hospitality involves caring for a guest's physical needs and listening to them, making sure that they feel valued for who they are.

Abba Poemen said,

> If a brother comes to visit you and you realise that you have not profited by his visit, search your heart, and discover what you were thinking about before he came, and then you will understand why his visit was useless.

> O God,
> make the door of this house wide enough

to receive all who need human love and fellowship,
and a heavenly Father's care;
   and narrow enough to shut out
all envy, pride and hate.
   Make its threshold smooth enough
to be no stumbling block to children,
nor to straying feet,
   but rugged enough to turn back
the tempter's power:
     make it a gateway
     to thine eternal kingdom.

*Bishop Thomas Ken*

READINGS FOR FURTHER MEDITATION

Genesis 18:1–8
Judges 6:11–23
Matthew 25:31–46
Mark 10:42–45
Luke 10:40–42
John 13:1–17
Hebrews 13:1–2
1 Peter 4:8–10
James 1:27

# WORK

Unless the Lord builds the house,
its builders will have toiled in vain

*Psalm 127*

*

## *Daily bread*

We have a duty to perform useful work. The Lord showed us
by His own example that work is a vital part of the human
vocation. Life comes to us only in return for effort – whether
this is the labour of bearing and educating children, or the
labour of production. It is your willingness to work which
makes your marriage possible, and which makes it possible for
you to found a family. Sometimes the work will be enjoyable,
sometimes disagreeable, or even painful, but always it is a
necessity. God's providence does not normally appear mira-
culously like manna from heaven: He provides for us through
our active cooperation with nature and one another. St Benedict reminds us that we cannot pretend to be Christians if we
are not willing to earn our daily bread (Rule Ch. 48). And St
Paul thought this was so important that he laid down this rule
for the earliest Christian communities: "the man who will not
work shall not eat" (2 Thessalonians 3:10).

Make sure, then, that you do not have a false spirituality
which sees work as demeaning: it is a noble activity, for when
we work we share in God's own creative power (which is why
Jesus called everything that He did "my Father's works").

145

F

The truly spiritual outlook is that which sees everything as coming from God's hands, everything as sanctified and holy – "we must not call unclean what God has made holy" (Acts 10:15).

## A school of work

Your marriage is a school of work, a place where you can learn the joy of working motivated by love and the desire to serve one another. When you work in this spirit your love for one another is made visible. It may be the work of creating a beautiful home, a place of welcome and peace for your spouse and for others; it may be the work of using your imagination, time and energy to care for the children born out of the committed love you have for each other; it may be work which earns money to support your family.

St Paul said, "acknowledge those who are working so hard among you" (1 Thessalonians 5:12). Work with the hands, work with the mind, and work with the spirit: all of these are real forms of labour. In many societies work in the home is not renumerated and is counted as less important than paid work; but the raising of a family is one of the greatest and most demanding of works. Show your appreciation, then, for your spouse's contribution to your marriage.

The Lord left us a living parable of His relationship to us: He washed His disciples' feet – the work of a slave in His time. He chose the lowliest and most menial of tasks and called all those baptised into Him to follow Him in this way of service. Your work of love, then, will rarely be either dramatic or out of the ordinary – it is more likely to be washing-up than washing feet – but by choosing to serve one another gladly in all that you do you will truly be following the Lord in His path to the Father.

## The spirit of work

"He is under the world's splendour and wonder", wrote Hopkins, "I greet him the days I meet him, and bless when I understand". What the Christian seeks is to find God in everything – in prayer, in work, in nature, and in other people. The Christian knows that there is no reality apart from God, Who fills all things with His presence. What makes any work Christian work, then, is not the type of work which is done, but the distinctive spirit in which it is performed. We do not work simply for ourselves or for others, but for God. As St Benedict says, we want God to be "glorified in everything".

If you do not put love into your work, offering it to God for His glory, then however important it may seem to be, it is worth nothing. Even if you earn a large salary, and have much influence in society, if you do not have love your work benefits no one. If love is not the foundation of your work and the motive for it, it is needless toil. But when you truly love, everything that you do and everything that you experience – difficult or easy, painful or joyful – is related to that love. And so your love for one another and for the Lord will penetrate and illuminate all your horizons, making even the most hidden and seemingly insignificant work shine with glory.

> Whatever you are doing, put your whole heart into it, as if you were doing it for the Lord and not for men.
>
> *Colossians 3:23*

## Hidden work

Much work is hidden from sight; unnoticed, it may be monotonous, and is certainly not glamorous. The ego, wanting to glory in its own achievements, resents this hiddenness; it wants others to see the work it has done. But if your work is like this you have the special privilege of following Jesus in His hidden years when, far from public view, He worked as an obscure carpenter in Nazareth. Much housework has this character, and those who perform it are indeed favoured by God. They are His "hidden ones" (Psalm 83:3), "hidden with Christ in God" (Colossians 3:2).

By steadfast dedication to the daily round, performed without fanfares or ostentation, you will come to value the greatest treasure in work: you will find your true self, the "inmost centre of your being, with its imperishable ornament, a gentle, quiet spirit" (1 Peter 3:4). For it is not our work which gives us value; it is *we* who give value to our work. It is because of our dignity as sons and daughters of God that even the smallest and seemingly most insignificant of actions has great importance in the eyes of God. So do not measure your value by what you do; measure the value of what you do by who you are – a redeemed child of God.

## A balanced life

St Benedict said that if any brother in the monastery needed extra help with a task, it should be provided, so that all work can be performed without any cause for grumbling. In the kitchen, for example, if there are extra guests the cook may need more help. St Benedict does not suggest that everybody in the community should try their hand at cooking – that might indeed be a cause for grumbling! – but that people should not rigidly stick to their own tasks and refuse to help others who obviously had problems.

This is good advice for married life as well. It is very easy to fall into a pattern of work that leaves one of the spouses constantly overburdened. So do not grudge each other your time and energy, but "bear one another's burdens" (Galatians 6:2).

Be sure to avoid activism: it is all too easy to exaggerate the importance of the work we are doing. Work must be harmonised with the other areas of your life. St Bernard pointed out that Martha and Mary are sisters and should not be enemies – they live together and support each other, and therefore work and rest should be balanced in our lives. In particular, keep the Lord's day as a time for rest and worship and for the joyful celebration of the presence of Christ in your marriage.

You have made us for yourself, O Lord, and our hearts are restless until they rest in you.

*St Augustine*


READINGS FOR FURTHER MEDITATION

Genesis 1:28
Proverbs 31:15–27
Matthew 6:25–34
Luke 10:38–42
1 Corinthians 13:1–8
2 Thessalonians 3:7–12

# PRAYER

If two of you agree on earth about any request you have
to make that request will be granted by my heavenly
Father

*Matthew 18:19*

*

### The Spirit will teach you

Prayer is a great privilege. It is the free invitation made to us
by God to share in His eternal communion. We do not have to
use prayer to take heaven by storm. Prayer is God: prayer is
the yearning of the Spirit, who came to live in our hearts at
baptism and now dwells within us, crying out "Abba, Father"
(Romans 8:15). Your task is to become aware of this prayer of
the Spirit, which is always bubbling up within you like a spring
of water. Your task is to allow the Spirit to teach you that the
Father is the source of your lives. Then you will come to
realise that your communion with each other in your marriage is grounded in the intimate life of the Father, Son and
Spirit, and that this is where you will find strength and new
life.

In prayer we try to forget ourselves and to be attentive to
God as the supreme reality. Coming from your time of prayer,
you will find that it deepens your conversion towards each
other as well. The essentials of prayer – an attitude of recep-
tiveness, a willingness to wait, a loving expectancy, an atten-
tiveness to the Other – are also the essentials of Christian

marriage, of the attitude you should have towards one another.

## Prayer and life

Your prayer and your life must never be separated. Christ's overriding concern was always to do the will of the Father (see John 4:34). This must be your concern as well, to say and to live "Your will be done in me". Let the desire for a closer union with God lead you to read the Scriptures and seek His word for you there; to pray in silence, being open to His mysterious presence; and to meditate on the salvation He won for you in Christ's death and resurrection.

Jesus said that you can always know a tree by its fruits (Matthew 7:20), and so you can know whether your prayer is authentically Christian by whether you are growing in love for one another, since this is the main fruit asked of you in marriage. This does not mean that you will always *feel* more loving towards one another, just as we do not necessarily experience God's love for us when we pray. God may be visiting the soul even when the experience in prayer is emptiness or affliction, for He may be inviting us to share more fully in Christ's own experience of abandonment in Gethsemene. The test is not what we feel and experience, but how we act. The crucial point is that you should be faithful in praying and in loving whatever you feel. Then you will be like the man praised by the psalmist:

> The law of the Lord is his delight,
> the law his meditation night and day.
> He is like a tree
> planted beside a watercourse,
> which yields its fruit in season

151

and its leaf never withers

*Psalm 1:2–3*

## *The rest of the soul*

St Benedict called prayer "Opus Dei", "the work of God". He knew that prayer is a task – the most useful and the most beautiful which God has given us to perform. What makes our active lives fruitful, said St Bernard, is the "rest" of the soul in the sweet embrace of God. If we do not give time to prayer, if we condemn it as mere idleness, or simply treat it as something expendable, then our lives – however useful they may seem to be – will only spread confusion and conflict.

The avoidance of prayer, said the Desert Fathers, is really a kind of sloth: we go to see people, we decide to organise things, to "get things done", we overload ourselves with work, and all this, not because we can really contribute very much, but because we cannot face the *effort* of staying still, of developing our interior life. And so Abba Agathon said, "There is no labour greater than prayer to God. For every time someone wants to pray, his enemies, the demons, want to prevent him, for they know that it is only by turning him from prayer that they can hinder his journey".

Although prayer seems to be a private matter, a point at which you withdraw from your marriage and seek some benefit just for yourself, you need a certain amount of solitude and prayer in order to love and value your spouse. Jesus said that He always prunes the fruitful branch so that it can bear more fruit (John 15:2) – He cuts us back and draws us away from too much activity so that we can nourish ourselves from His life. When you experience the love God has for you, you will be set free to care for each other, and not simply use each other for your own support and comfort. And so St

152

Bernard wrote, "I seem to have been led in alone, but it does not profit me alone. Every preferment of mine is also yours".

## *Never alone*

Even in solitude Christians never pray alone. All Christian prayer shares in the longing of the Church, of the bride who thirsts for her Lord, saying "Come, Lord Jesus" (Revelation 22:20). Therefore, Jesus taught His disciples to say *"Our* Father", and "forgive us *our* sins", rather than "my Father" and "my sins", and He said that where two or three were gathered to pray in His name, He was in their midst. Pray as a couple, then, standing together to worship God. Love and make your own the prayers of the Church which have served generations of believers, especially the rosary and the Divine Office.

If at all possible, begin the day with prayer, for "if the root is consecrated, so are the branches" (Romans 11:16). Offer your marriage to God, asking that He will work in it according to His will. And end each day with prayer, thanking God for each other and giving yourselves into His hands: "For you alone, Lord, make us dwell in safety" (Psalm 4:8).

## *Our Lady and St Joseph*

Dedicate your marriage to the Blessed Virgin and to St Joseph, who are your models and guardians, and your teachers in the way of prayer.

St Joseph is above all a man of faith. In his own life he was severely tempted to distrust God, to disbelieve the good news of God's Son taking flesh in Mary's womb: was Mary's child *really* of the Holy Spirit? In many icons of the Nativity, St Joseph is shown sitting apart from the main group, tempted by

Satan, who is casting doubt on the miracle of the Incarnation. As a constant friend, St Joseph will teach you that your marriage, like the Church herself, is based on the miraculous. Without faith in the living God, for Whom nothing is impossible, your prayer will be meaningless.

The Mother of the Redeemer wants us to share in her own maternity, to receive Christ in the depths of our hearts as she did in her flesh. She wants the Lord Jesus to be born and conceived in us until, as Aelred of Rievaulx says, "we all come to perfect manhood, that maturity which is proportioned to the complete growth in Christ". At every moment the Spirit is prompting you to say "yes" to the birth of Christ in your marriage.

There is no technique which needs to be learned. Prayer, like marriage, is a personal relationship based on freedom. Mary wants you to be completely abandoned to God, saying with her "Let it be done to us according to your will". Most of the time we lack Mary's simplicity. We argue with God; we evade, hesitate and procrastinate; we make alternative suggestions. Mary's "yes", uncomplicated as a shaft of sunlight, does not come easy to us. But what matters, as Jesus' parable of the two sons shows us, is that we do eventually say "yes" (Matthew 21:28–32).

"To this day", writes Guerric of Igny, "we remain in the shelter of the mother of the Most High, remaining under her protection as it were under the shadow of her wings. And in the days to come we shall share in her glory; we shall know the warmth of her loving embrace. Then there will be one joyful voice proclaiming the praise of our mother: Holy Mother of God, in you we all find our home".

## *The Sufficient Place*

See, all the silver roads wind in, lead in
To this still place like evening. See, they come
Like messengers bearing gifts to this little house,
And this great hill worn down to a patient mound,
And these tall trees whose motionless branches bear
An aeon's summer foliage, leaves so thick
They seem to have robbed a world of shade, and kept
No room for all these birds that line the boughs
With heavier riches, leaf and bird and leaf.
   Within the doorway stand
Two figures, Man and Woman, simple and clear
As a child's first images. Their manners are
Such as were known before the earliest fashion
Taught the Heavens guile. The room inside is like
A thought that needed thus much space to write on,
Thus much, no more. Here all's sufficient. None
That comes complains, and all the world comes here,
Comes, and goes out again, and comes again.
This is the Pattern, these the Archetypes,
Sufficient, strong, and peaceful. All outside
From end to the end of the world is tumult. Yet
These roads do not turn in here but writhe on
Round the wild earth for ever. If a man
Should chance to find this place three times in time
His eyes are changed and make a summer silence
Amid the tumult, seeing the roads wind in
To their still home, the house and the leaves and birds.

*Edwin Muir*

READINGS FOR FURTHER MEDITATION

Psalm 1
Matthew 18:19–20
Luke 11:1–13
Ephesians 3:14–21

# COMMUNICATING

I have called you my beloved, for I revealed to you
everything.

*John 15:15*

\*

*Truth is your rule of life*

Jesus is called the "Word of God" because He is God's
communication to us. He is the entire truth of who God is for
us, since in Him "the complete being of God, by God's own
choice, came to dwell" (Colossians 1:19). As God's Word,
Jesus is the guarantee of God's faithfulness to us: God shows
that He can always be trusted to do what He says by making
His Word become flesh in the person of Jesus (John 1:14).

Jesus perfectly communicates the truth of God's love for
us. There are no secrets between Christ and His bride: He
knows us through and through – "I know whom I have
chosen" (John 13:8); and on the other hand He reveals to
us everything about the Father, the innermost source of His
life.

In the same way, make sure that there are no areas of your
life which remain secret and hidden from one another, but
share with each other your weaknesses as well as your
strengths. When you married, a spiritual bond was formed
between you and you became guardians of one another's
souls. The Lord has entrusted you to each other's care. Allow
your spouse to know you and to care for you, then, and never

try to overcome problems on your own, or you will be departing from this path of two-in-one.

> Truth is the rule of life for all of you
>> *St Ignatius of Antioch*

## Making time for each other

Intimacy in marriage does not develop automatically; neither does it remain without some effort – in some marriages one can see how close friends have become strangers over time, while in others relative strangers have become the closest of friends. The engagement period is often a time when couples share with each other on a very deep and personal level, and Old Testament law laid it down that newlyweds should be relieved of their normal obligations in society for a year to allow them to spend time together, and nourish their marriage on frequent communication (see Deuteronomy 24:5).

Make sure, then, that you have a regular time set apart when you can simply be together, to talk about things that are important to you and about your feelings, as well as about day-to-day affairs. It is a commonplace to note how television, videos and home computers can substitute passive entertainment in the home for authentic human contact. But it is not any less true for being commonplace. It is not rare now to go into homes where the family does not even "meet" around the television – each member of the family has his or her own set and watches it in private. Do not allow your time for personal communication to be eroded – by television, leisure activities, or even by your work: a lasting and rewarding unity will only be formed in your marriage through time being given to be with one another.

## Soul-friends

A friend loves at all times
*Proverbs 17:17*

A marriage should be a place where we are enabled to communicate, first of all, with *ourselves*. It can be alarming to realise how much that we know to be true about ourselves we manage to hide among convenient shadows in the recesses of the mind. We need assistance in opening ourselves up to the truth about ourselves and in coming to a realistic and mature self-acceptance.

It is a spouse who is truly a soul-friend, who is completely committed to loving you, who can give you the confidence and encouragement to be more open to life, more willing to receive truth and to have the courage to live by what you see. Be soul-friends to each other, then, so that your spouse can feel relaxed and secure enough to tell you about their ideas, their hopes and fears, their embarrassments and their joys. What is needed is a deep, loving acceptance of them as they are – which does not mean either a blindness to their faults or a condescending pity. Thomas Merton wrote,

> In the long run, no one can show another the error that is within him, unless the other is convinced that his critic first sees and loves the good that is within him . . . Love . . . this alone can open the door to truth.

## Bringing life or death

Where there is no vision the people perish
*Proverbs 29:18*

159

St Benedict warned his monks repeatedly against complaining, moaning, and judging others. He knew that nothing destroys a community as quickly as this. Cynical talk, and words used to wound another, should also be outlawed from the monastery.

The person who is able to control his speech, said St James, is perfect and is in full control of his being (James 3:2). The Lord told His disciples that this control begins in our thoughts, in the silences of the heart: it is here that sincere love is born, or that judging and criticising begin. A genuine power is attributed to thought and speech in the Scriptures: God's word can create life (Genesis 1:1ff), and can break open our hearts in a healing sorrow at our sins (Hosea 6:5).

In the same way, our words can bring life to others if they are rooted in God's vision of the world. Thinking and speaking in a positive way can create a positive reality, just as thinking and speaking bitterly and negatively can harm and distort others. If you keep in your heart a vision of your spouse in all their beauty, seeing them as God sees them – their glory not shrouded and disfigured by sin – and if you relate to them in the light of this vision, then your spouse can more easily become what you see that they are in their deepest being. This is not magic or a technique. It is the power of the love which is behind the vision and within the words you speak. The love needed for you to persevere in holding this vision of your spouse is itself a great gift from God, but it is given as soon as you say "yes" to God's word being spoken in your life.

## Forgiveness

I have never gone to sleep with a grievance against anyone, and, as far as I could, I have never let anyone go to sleep with a grievance against me.  *Abba Agathon*

In this life, thought St Augustine, our righteousness consists more in the forgiveness of sins than in the perfection of our virtues; and so a truly Christian marriage is not one where conflict is absent, but one in which forgiveness is evident. God sent His Son into the world to reconcile the world to Himself, not counting our sins against us. God has taken the initiative, and has given us this same ministry of reconciliation.

The Lord tells us that we must actively seek reconciliation with each other: "If, when you are bringing your gift to the altar, you suddenly remember that your brother has a grievance against you, leave your gift where it is before the altar. First go and make your peace with your brother; and only then come back and offer your gift" (Matthew 5:23–24). Cassian comments on this in the following way,

> the common Lord of all does not care so much for our homage as to lose in one what He gains in another ... For in anyone's loss He suffers some loss, who desires and looks for the salvation of all His servants in one and the same way.

So, then, make sure that there is no barrier between you. Forgiveness does not mean minimising what has happened, but letting go of the past. When you forgive you enable one another to make a fresh start with new hope. And because we are always sinners Christ said that there should be no limit to our forgiveness, just as God is unlimited in His mercy towards us (Matthew 18:21–22). And, through God's grace, you will find that as you forgive each other all that is negative in your marriage will become the means of a greater depth of unity between you: in Christ every "no" of sin is pulled into His victory on the Cross, where it becomes a fuller occasion for His own "yes" to God. So do not allow anger to remain in your hearts, but speak to one another, always seeking peace and reconciliation. Never lose sight of the mercy of God, and show that mercy to each other.

It is no small consolation in this life to have someone you can unite with you in an intimate affection and the embrace of a holy love, someone in whom your spirit can rest, to whom you can pour out your soul, to whose pleasant exchanges, as to soothing songs, you can fly in sorrow, to the dear breast of whose friendship, amidst the many troubles of this world, you can safely retire, to whose loving heart, as to yourself, you can unhesitatingly commit the stomach of all your thoughts; with whose spiritual kisses, as with remedial salves, you may draw out all the weariness of your restless anxieties. A man who can shed tears with you in your worries, be happy with you when things go well, search out with you the answers to your problems, whom with the ties of charity you can lead into the depths of your heart.

*Aelred of Rievaulx*

READINGS FOR FURTHER MEDITATION

Genesis 1:1–31
Ecclesiasticus 6:14–17
Matthew 5:7
Colossians 3:8–11

# NOTES

## Chosen by God

St Bernard of Clairvaux: *Sermons on the Song of Songs* 84:5

## The Other as the basis of Existence

St Bernard of Clairvaux: *On Loving God*

Henri de Lubac: *Catholicism* (Burns, Oates and Washbourne 1950) p. 181

St Bernard of Clairvaux on the visitations of God: *Sermons on the Song of Songs* 57

Edwin Muir: *Collected Poems* (Faber and Faber 1960) p. 122

St John of the Cross: *Living Flame of Love* Stanza III

## The Image of God in Marriage

Pope John Paul II: *The Christian Family in the Modern World* (1981) paragraph 11

St John Chrysostom: both quotations are taken from his *Homily 20 on Ephesians 5:22–33*

St Augustine: *The Trinity* 8:8:12

St Gregory of Nyssa: quoted in Pope John Paul II: *The Dignity and Vocation of Women* (1989) note 25

## The Gift of Self

St Basil the Great: *Epistle 38*

St Benedict: *Rule* Chapter 33

Heloise: quoted in B. Radice (trans): *The Letters of Abelard and Heloise* (Penguin 1974) p. 117

Pachomius: quoted in P. Rousseau: *Pachomius* (University of California Press 1985) p. 97

## Unity is Your Vocation

St Cyril of Alexandria: quoted in Henri de Lubac: *ibid* p. 7
St Augustine: *The Trinity* 4:9
St Ignatius of Antioch: *Epistle to Polycarp*
St John Chrysostom: *Homily 12 on Colossians 4:18*
St Dorotheus of Gaza: in E.P. Wheeler (trans): *Dorotheus of Gaza* (Cistercian Publications 1977) p. 252
St Gregory of Nyssa: *Homilies on the Song of Songs* 15

## Choices

St Benedict: *Rule* Chapter 4
St Leo the Great: *Sermon II, 1*
St John of the Cross: *The Ascent of Mount Carmel* 1:10
A Cistercian monk: quoted in B.P. McGuire: *Friendship and Community: The Monastic Experience 350–1250* (Cistercian Publications 1988) p. 371

## Vowing

St Benedict, on full knowledge and freedom in vowing: *Rule* Chapter 58
St Francis de Sales: *The Devout Life* Part 3, Chapter 38
William of St Thierry: *The Golden Epistle* paragraph 16

## Stability

St Benedict on gyrovagues: *Rule* Chapter 1; on the endurance of the true monk: *Rule* Chapter 7
The monk in trouble: *Patrologia Latina VII* 34, col. 901

## Conversion

Abba Poemen: in Benedicta Ward (trans): *The Sayings of the Desert Fathers* (Mowbrays 1975) p. 179
St Benedict: *Rule* prologue
St Augustine: *City of God* 22:30

William of St Thierry: *The Golden Epistle* paragraph 38
Abba Anthony: in Benedicta Ward: *Ibid* p. 185
St Ignatius of Antioch: *Epistle to the Ephesians*
St Cyprian of Carthage: *Epistle* 46
St Augustine: *Confessions* 7:26–27

## Obedience

St Irenaeus: *Against Heresies* 5:1:3
St Augustine: *On True Religion* 69
St Bernard of Clairvaux: *The Steps of Humility and Pride* 3:7
St Augustine: *Exposition on Psalm 70*
St Dorotheus of Gaza: E.P. Wheeler: *Ibid* p. 239

## You are a Sacrament

Vatican II: *The Church in the Modern World* paragraph 48

## The Mystery of Marriage

Rainer Maria Rilke: *Letters* (New York 1945) 12 February 1902
*The Cloud of Unknowing*: Chapter 6
St Augustine: *Confessions* 10:8

## The Presence of God

Abba Paul: in Benedicta Ward: *Ibid* p. 205
St Irenaeus: *Against Heresies* 3:24
St Augustine: the first quotation is taken from his *Confessions* 5:2;
    the second is from his *Rule* section 2
Amma Syncletica: in Benedicta Ward: *Ibid* p. 233

## A Place of Salvation

St Benedict: *Rule* Chapter 28
St Augustine: *Confessions* 10:39
St Anthony: in Benedicta Ward: *Ibid* p. 2
St John Chrysostom: *Homily 20 on Ephesians 5:22–33*

The saying about hell is from Macarius the Great, which can be found in Benedicta Ward: *Ibid* pp. 115–116

George MacDonald: *Unspoken Sermons, 3rd Series: "Freedom"* (Longman Green 1899)

## One Flesh

St John of Damascus: *First Homily in Defence of the Holy Icons*
St Ignatius of Antioch: *Epistle to the Ephesians*
St Thomas Aquinas: *Summa Theologica* I, 98, 2 ad 3

## On Guarding the Heart Against Evil Thoughts

The eight kinds of evil thoughts are listed in Evagrius: *The Praktikos* 6 and Cassian: *The Institutes* 5:1

Both sayings of Abba Poemen are from Benedicta Ward: *Ibid* p. 143

St Ignatius of Loyola describes the devil as an army commander in his *Spiritual Exercises* paragraph 327

St Hesychios: "On Watchfulness and Holiness": 84, from G.E.H. Palmer, P. Sherrard and K. Ware (trans): *The Philokalia* Vol. 1 (Faber and Faber 1979)

St Benedict: *Rule* Chapters 4 and 50

Evagrius: *The Praktikos* 33

Cassian: *The Institutes* 4:9

The story of John the Dwarf is from Benedicta Ward: *Ibid* p. 75

Aelred of Rievaulx: *Pastoral Prayer* 8

## Doubt

"He knows all . . .": A Monk: *The Hermitage Within* (DLT 1977) p. 16

St Athanasius: *The Life of St. Anthony* chapters 27–30

## Anger

Cassian: the quotations are from *The Institutes* 8:1, 14, 17

St Isaiah the Solitary: "On Guarding the Intellect", in Palmer et al.: *Ibid*

St Dorotheus of Gaza: Maxims on the Spiritual Life no. 17, and extracts from "On Self-accusation" in E.P. Wheeler: *Ibid*

St John of the Cross: *Counsels of Light and Love* (Burns and Oates 1977) p. 65

## Discouragement

Abba Apollo: in N. Russell (trans): *Lives of the Desert Fathers* (Mowbray 1981) VIII: 52–3

Abba Poemen: in Benedicta Ward: *Ibid* p. 151

St Benedict: on tiredness, *Rule* Chapter 64; on God's grace, the prologue

St John of Karpathos: "Texts for the monks in India", in Palmer et al.: *Ibid* p. 306

Evagrius: *The Praktikos* 10

## The Desire to Dominate

St Augustine: *City of God* 19:12

St Bernard of Clairvaux: *Sermons on the Song of Songs* 49:7

Aelred of Rievaulx: *Spiritual Friendship* 1:57

St Gregory Nazianzen: *Or. 43*

St Augustine: *The Ways of the Catholic Church* 1:33:73

## Living Simply

St Bernard of Clairvaux: *Sermons on the Song of Songs* 71

St Augustine: *Sermon on Psalm 147*

Richard of St Victor: *The Trinity* III: 4 and 6

Abba Poemen: from Benedicta Ward: *Ibid* p. 147

William of St Thierry: *Meditations* 12:14

St Cyprian of Carthage: *On Works and Alms*

St John Chrysostom: *In Inscriptionem Altaris et in Principium Adorum* 1:2

St Benedict: *Rule* Chapter 31

## Hospitality

St Benedict: *Rule* Chapter 53
Abba James: in Benedicta Ward: *Ibid* p. 89
St Bernard of Clairvaux: *Sermons on the Song of Songs* 18
Story of hermit: *Patrologia Latina XII* 7, Col. 943
Abba Poeman: in Benedicta Ward: *Ibid* p. 161

## Work

G.M. Hopkins: *The Wreck of the Deutschland*
St Benedict: "That God may be glorified in everything", *Rule* Chapter 57; on providing extra help, *Rule* Chapter 53
St Bernard of Clairvaux: see *Thomas Merton on St. Bernard* (Cistercian Publications 1980) pp. 42f
St Augustine: *Confessions* 1:1

## Prayer

Abba Agathon: in Benedicta Ward: *Ibid* p. 18
St Bernard of Clairvaux: *Sermons on the Song of Songs* 23
Aelred of Rievaulx: *Jesus at the Age of Twelve* 4
Guerric of Igny: *Homily 1 on Mary's Assumption*
Edwin Muir: *Collected Poems* (Faber and Faber 1960) pp. 86–7

## Communicating

St Ignatius of Antioch: *Epistle to the Ephesians*
Thomas Merton: *Conjectures of a Guilty Bystander* (Burns and Oates 1968) pp. 56f
St Benedict on complaining: *Rule* Chapters 34, 35, 40, 41, 53
Abba Agathon: in Benedicta Ward: *Ibid* p. 18
St Augustine: *City of God* 19:27
Cassian: *Institutes* 8:14
Aelred of Rievaulx: *Mirror of Charity* 3:39